THE FOUNDATIONS
OF LANGUAGE

THE FOUNDATIONS
OF LANGUAGE

Talking and Reading in Young Children

by

ANDREW WILKINSON

Reader in Education in English
School of Education, University of Birmingham

OXFORD UNIVERSITY PRESS

1971

Oxford University Press, Ely House, London W.1

GLASGOW NEW YORK TORONTO MELBOURNE WELLINGTON
CAPE TOWN SALISBURY IBADAN NAIROBI DAR ES SALAAM LUSAKA ADDIS ABABA
BOMBAY CALCUTTA MADRAS KARACHI LAHORE DACCA
KUALA LUMPUR SINGAPORE HONG KONG TOKYO

For DAVID
and HELEN

PRINTED AND BOUND IN ENGLAND BY
HAZELL WATSON AND VINEY LTD
AYLESBURY, BUCKS

ACKNOWLEDGEMENTS

It is impossible to acknowledge all one's debts in a book of this kind. Working in an academic climate one assimilates ideas often without being aware of their source: sometimes a single remark or comment from a colleague, on some other issue entirely, illuminates the problems pre-occupying one's mind. However, I am particularly conscious of my debt to the seminal work of two people – M. A. K. Halliday, and Basil Bernstein. Even where I may disagree with them their influence on my thinking will nevertheless be apparent to the reader of this book.

The climate of ideas provided by one's colleagues in the University of Birmingham owes a good deal to such people as John Sinclair, of the English department; and Leslie Stratta, with whom many valuable discussions have taken place in the Oracy Research Unit of the School of Education. R. Gulliford has been particularly helpful on the topic of reading, Michael Tobin on the language of the blind, Jim Wight on the language of West Indian immigrants, S. Clague-Smith on Swahili. E. Stones has kindly given permission for me to quote him on concept formation. Pauline Roberts, Secretary of the Oracy Research Unit in the School of Education, has made a valued contribution not only in typing a difficult manuscript but in skilled editing of a large number of tapes.

But the chief acknowledgement should go to the young children whose words are quoted fully and frequently, particularly to Guy Leach, David McGeogh, Andrew McGeogh, Edmund Russell, and Helen Wilkinson. Without them the book would not have been possible.

A.M.W.
Barnt Green, Worcs.
June, 1970.

CONTENTS

8   CONTENTS

CHAPTER II – LANGUAGE AND SITUATION

CHAPTER III – THE ACQUISITION OF LANGUAGE

CONTENTS

CONTENTS

CONTENTS

CHAPTER I

THE ELEMENTS OF LANGUAGE

1. *WHAT IS LANGUAGE?*

In Aldous Huxley's *Crome Yellow* (Chapter V) the old farm labourer Rowley draws attention to his pigs: 'Look at them, sir,' he said, with a motion of his hand towards the wallowing swine. 'Rightly is they called pigs.'

This is of course a naïve assumption – that the names of things belong essentially to them as do their colour, size, and shape. A moment's reflection will show us that this is not true; for instance, the names will be different in other languages. The French even have the temerity to use the letters of *pain* to mean bread. Words are in fact arbitrary: that is to say there is no reason why one should be used rather than another except by common agreement of speakers of the language, the 'language community' as we call it. There is no reason why the star we call the 'sun' should not be called the 'moon'; and if everybody agreed, this could be done tomorrow. When women change their names on marriage there is a common agreement to accept the new name. And names, words in general, are sounds. These sounds stand for, or symbolize, objects, processes, relationships. 'The elephant is smoking a pipe' symbolizes for the listener, or reader, an event which he is probably not witnessing. Words can also be symbolized by combinations of letters, but these are secondary, being in origin attempts to write down the sounds. We may say then that language is primarily a system of agreed sounds.

Now animals make noises which are 'agreed sounds', in the sense that animals know, as *though* by agreement, what they mean. We may instance the mating, territorial, and alarm calls of birds. But these are instinctive; and the reaction of other creatures to them is also instinctive. They are in fact incapable of coming to an agreement that a particular sound is to have a particular meaning. Human beings make instinctive noises – a grunt, a cry of pain, for example, but these are part and parcel of the exertion or emotion itself, rather than voluntarily chosen symbols for it. Language differs from such animal noises in being non-instinctive; if it were instinctive then there would only be one language, and the large variety of languages in the world would not exist. Again, animal sounds cannot be arranged in relation to one another. The song-thrush cannot put his mating call in conjunction with his alarm call to mean 'I love you, but you frighten me to death,' but we, by using verbal symbols, have just done so. We are thus in a position to understand Sapir's (1921) definition: 'Language is a purely human and non-instinctive method of communicating ideas, emotions, and desires, by means of a system of voluntarily produced symbols.'

2. *WHAT LANGUAGE DO WE SPEAK?*

The reader of this book probably speaks, he can certainly read –

1. A language from the Indo-European families of world languages.
2. English.
3. A dialect of English.
4. An idiolect of English.
5. A register of English.

2.1 AN INDO-EUROPEAN LANGUAGE

English belongs to the Indo-European family of world languages. There are other language families – for instance, there is a Semitic group to which Hebrew and Arabic belong; and others, including Chinese, which are quite unrelated to Indo-European or to one another. In Indo-European there are subdivisions, the main ones being: Teutonic (English, German, Dutch, the Scandinavian languages); Italic (Latin – French, Spanish, Italian); Hellenic (Classical Greek – Modern Greek); Celtic (Gaelic, Irish, Welsh); Slavonic (Russian, etc.); and Indian (Hindi, etc.). The original language from which all these are descended was spoken some time before 2000 B.C., possibly round about 3000 or 4000 B.C., by people living, it is conjectured, in Northern or Central Europe. There are no written records of this language, but scholars infer its existence from evidence such as the similarity of words in modern languages:

English	German	Dutch	Swedish	Danish /	Latin	French /	Greek
one	ein	een	en	een	unus	un	oinos

The similarities in one sub-group are closer that those between sub-groups, but all are too close for coincidence. Nor can we explain the similarities as due to borrowing at a later date. There would be no contact between some of the peoples concerned at the time when their languages were developing.

That languages may come from a common stock is not merely of scholarly and historical interest. The evidence suggests that the closer a language is to one's own, the easier it is to learn. Chinese, belonging to a different language group, is very hard for a native English speaker.

2.2 THE ENGLISH LANGUAGE

English is an international language, the most widespread in the world, second only to Mandarin Chinese in the number who speak it. After Chinese and English follow Hindi, Russian, Spanish, German, Japanese, French, Malay, Bengali, Arabic, Portuguese and Italian in that order (Potter 1968). English is spoken as a first language in England, U.S.A., Canada, New Zealand, Australia, and by some people of European stock in parts of Africa. It is natural that these speakers should introduce variations in it, and we shall be looking at these. For the moment let us look at what they have in common.

Saussure, the French linguist (1857–1913), introduced a distinction which will help us here, a distinction between 'language' (*langue*) and 'speech' (*parole*). 'Parole' is the way words are spoken, in a variety of different circumstances, by a variety of different people. But 'langue' is the basic system which they interpret for themselves: 'langue' is 'not a function of the speaker: it is a product that is passively assimilated by the individual . . . speaking, on the contrary, is an individual act' (Saussure, p. 14). What Saussure means by 'langue' is the kind of concept we have in mind when we speak of 'the English language' – rather than any particular manifestation of it as 'parole' in speech (or writing).

The English language in this sense has three parts: one consists of the sounds we make when pronouncing it, its phonology; the second consists of a large number of words, which we call 'vocabulary' or 'lexis'; the third consists of a number of rules, which we call 'grammar', for joining these words together in groups and sentences. The native speaker is not usually conscious of these rules: he just uses them, and even the most uneducated speaker uses them, in the main, acceptably. It is those times when he does not that mark him out as an uneducated speaker (see Ch. VII, 1.1.); when, for instance, he says *I done it* instead of *I did it*. Even here he is communicating effectively, in that the listener does not doubt his meaning.

We have spoken of some forms of English as being 'acceptable'. And the question immediately arises: acceptable to whom? The answer is: acceptable to the international community of educated speakers of the language. We cannot speak of some usages as being 'incorrect' in the sense that '2 + 2 = 5' is incorrect. Over many centuries conventions have grown up about what are, and what are not, acceptable usages. They are conventions and not eternal laws. If the international community of educated speakers decided tomorrow that they preferred *I done it*, then *I done it* would become the accepted form. What we call 'standard English' is an English that observes these conventions.

Many of the 'mis-usages' which raise such a furore in the

correspondence columns of local newspapers are trivial; they are often perfectly acceptable in any case. Some of the trouble stems from the work of early grammarians who tried to make English fit rules derived from Latin and Greek. Churchill's reprimand to the clerk who altered one of his prepositions ('This is the sort of interference up with which I will not put') may have put an end to the pedantry (started by Dryden) which insists that we must not end a sentence with a preposition. The bane of the purist is the split infinitive. Certainly it may sometimes sound inelegant: *I am going to definitely repeat the exercise*, for instance. But on other occasions – *to definitely decide*, for example – it seems to give more emphasis. And in some cases, as in *to really try*, it is unavoidable. Bernard Shaw wrote to *The Times* in about 1907: 'There is a busybody on your staff who devotes a lot of time to chasing split infinitives. Every good literary craftsman splits his infinitives when the sense demands it. I call for the immediate dismissal of this pedant. It is of no consequence whether he decides to go quickly, or quickly to go, or to quickly go. The important thing is that he should go at once.' (It should be noted incidentally that Shaw uses another of the purist's aversions: *a lot of* for *much*.)

We cannot object to usages in English on the grounds that they would not occur in classical languages. Nor can we do so on the grounds of logic. Many people would prefer 'different from' to 'different to', arguing that the words imply an opposition; on the other hand, the same people might well use 'averse to' though 'averse from' might seem more logical. Nor can we object to grammatical usages on historical grounds. Language changes, and a form like *ain't*, which was perfectly acceptable in the nineteenth century for the first person singular, is no longer so today. The only standard, as we have seen, is the usage of the community of educated speakers.

2.3 DIALECT

So far we have spoken of phonology, lexis, and grammar. When the term 'standard English' is employed by linguists in the

U.K. they nowadays use it to refer to the second two only; but the layman may well include the first also; for him a 'standard-English speaker' may refer to someone having a particular accent. It is, however, useful for us to keep the distinction in this discussion of dialect.

2.3.1 REGIONAL DIALECT

When we speak of a dialect we commonly mean a form of English – lexis and grammar – spoken in a particular region. Thus in this sense the standard English of the U.K. and the standard English of the U.S.A. are both dialects of English; they will differ in certain details of lexis (*trash can/dust-bin; elevator/lift; sidewalk/pavement*) and grammar (*got/gotten; dived/dove* – northern but not southern U.S.A.). However, they are much closer to each other than to other dialects spoken in the two countries, and in fact we do not usually call them 'dialects', a term reserved for forms of English differing from them in the respective countries.

In England the term 'dialect' is usually applied to regional varieties, which are rapidly disappearing as social mobility and education increase, and the older speakers die out. But in Lancashire and Yorkshire, for instance, in many other parts of the country, local forms can still be heard: *theh, tha/thou; nobbut/nothing but; skrike/cry; laik/play*; and many more. Such speakers would probably switch to a more standard usage with speakers from another part of the country. But in fact in England standard English originated as a regional dialect. English was brought over by the Angles, Saxons, and Jutes, and as they settled in different parts of the country, over a period of time their forms of English, and their pronunciation of them, began to vary. The dialect of south-east England, because it was in use in London and the court, was probably more generally comprehensible as a middle dialect; and because books began to be written in it, became accepted as standard.

Let us now turn to the way the dialect (i.e. the grammar and lexis) is pronounced, for dialects often have a pronunciation or 'accent' associated with them. Educated English speakers the world over tend to speak a standard lexis and grammar, but their accents may vary with their origins, depending on whether they come from Texas, New England, Devon, or Lancashire, for example. In both the U.K. and the U.S.A. certain accents have high prestige: the educated pronunciation of a speaker from Illinois and that of one from the Home Counties (round London) are instances; but in the U.S.A. accents seem less rigidly ranked in order of precedence than in the U.K., though there are many unacceptable accents.

The regional basis of many accents can be best seen in the work of the dialect geographers, who use the techniques of meteorology, for instance, to draw lines or *isoglosses* on maps, demarking the occurrence of a particular feature of pronunciation (or, for that matter, of grammar or lexis). Thus the word *the*, which is spoken in full in most English dialects, becomes in various parts of Lancashire and Yorkshire *t* before consonants and vowels: *t'book*, *t'apple* (or *t'* (glottal stop) *apple*); or *t* before consonants, *t'book* and *th* before vowels *th'apple*; or is not pronounced, *he took book* (there are also other refinements) (Jones, in Robins, 1964, p. 54). In the north-west midlands, especially south Lancashire and Sheffield, a word like *tongue* receives a heavy pronunciation of the g (*ng*) as against a lighter one (ŋ) elsewhere (see the map in Brook, 1963, p. 95). A common indicator of north/south is the short vowel in words like *laugh*, *path*, in the north, as against the long one in the south. Of course, accent differences are not just a matter of the pronunciation of individual sounds – there are more general phonological differences, differences of 'sentence tune' For instance, speakers from the west midlands – the 'Black Country' – tend to use a rising intonation towards the end of their sentences. (See 3.1 below for discussion of phonology.) There is an English Dialects Survey in progress, directed from Leeds University; and various linguistic atlases for parts of the U.S., details of which can be found in a useful introduction to U.S. dialects by Malstrom and Ashley (1963).

Linguistically no accents are superior to any others. As long as effective communication is going on, the linguist does not pass judgement on aesthetic merits; he does not accept that some accents are intrinsically 'beautiful' and some are 'ugly' and 'slovenly'. Nevertheless, it is certainly true that some accents have more prestige than others. It has been suggested (Wilkinson, 1965) that in the U.K. there is a heirarchy of accents: first-class (R.P. = Received Pronunciation (that of a B.B.C. announcer), a form of Scots, Southern Irish, and certain foreign accents); second-class (most regional accents); and third-class (industrial and town accents). In a valuable piece of work Giles (1970) shows the picture to be more complex than this, but confirms the general outlines. He finds that no accent ranks equal with R.P., but that French and North American foreign accents were afforded higher status than British regional accents. Town and industrial accents have lowest status. One of Giles's tests was to ask his judges to rate accents from recordings. The 'status content' ranking was: 1. R.P., 2. Affected R.P., 3. North American and French, 5. German, 6. Southern Welsh, 7. Irish, 8. Italian, 9. Northern English, 10. Somerset 11. Indian and Cockney, 13. Birmingham. It is interesting that the Birmingham accent should be ranked even lower than that of an immigrant group such as the Indians. In another of Giles's scales – when the judges were asked to rank accents in status order *on paper* – both West Indian and Indian were of low prestige, but higher than Birmingham.

2.3.2 SOCIAL DIALECT

So far we have ostensibly been writing about regional dialects, but it will not have escaped the reader's notice that a social aspect enters into our discussion: class as well as geography to consider. Indeed, the concern of educationists recently has rather been with 'social dialects' than with regional ones. Such social dialects differ both in character and pronunciation from the standard language. In the U.K. it is still possible to consider the standard language of certain 'lower-working-class' groups as being a more restricted form of English than the standard.

But the arrival of immigrants, such as those from the West Indies, whose English may have significant differences from this standard, causes the British to think again about the nature of social dialect. However, in the United States, with three main standard dialects, northern, midland, and southern, there is a large number of non-standard dialects – partly because of the different national origins of the speakers – and this problem has been of great educational concern for many years. Thus there are many varieties of non-standard Negro speech, deriving originally, it seems, from rural southern dialects, but now used in many urban areas in the south and west. Stewart describes a continuum of language learnt in the American home from standard English, through the dialect of, for example, a lower-class white of the South Atlantic coast, a lower-class Negro of the same area, and a Jamaican creole speaker, to that of a Portuguese, those at the lower end requiring at least some foreign-language teaching procedures (Stewart, 1964, p. 11). A continuum with fewer steps, reaching from British standard English to the native Hindi of the Indian immigrant, could be drawn from the U.K. McDavid (1967) finds it possible to generalize about non-standard dialects in the U.S.A, as regards both pronunciation and language, to the extent of producing a check-list of significant features.

A brief indication of some of the problems of a speaker with non-standard dialect in face of the standard form can be gathered from a brief description of Jamaican Creole. This is a language developed by West Africans taken to the West Indies as slaves in the seventeenth and eighteenth centuries into a context where English was the prestige language, as a result of interaction between English and their native languages.

A sentence in Jamaican Creole (there are other forms of Creole) could be:

im	sel	mi	di	manggo-dem	yeside
he	sold	me	the	mangoes	yesterday

im: he, she, or it.

sel: no alteration for past tense; alternatively, past could be indicated by the word *en-en sel.*

    no agreement between subject and verb—contrast *he sells* in English.

mi: me (or I); cf. *wi* (we or us).

di: the

manggo-dem.: singular *manggo,* made plural by adding the particle *dem.*

yeside: yesterday; this is the only word indicating that the action took place in the past.

Certain features of the language are illustrated in the sentence. The tense system is undeveloped compared with that of English, the verb lacks time reference and we commonly have to gather the tense from the context. To some extent we can do this in English (cp. *I am taking the examination tomorrow,* where the verb is present but the future is indicated by *to-morrow*). There is no agreement between subject and verb (cp. non-standard English *I sells, he sells, they sells*). Personal pronouns have no cases (but the second person has a distinction between singular and plural, *you/unu,* which English once had, *thou/you*). There is no gender in the third person, and we have to deduce from the context. Plurals in nouns, usually indicated by the addition of *s* in English, are indicated by the addition of *-dem* in Creole, except with mass nouns, referring to non-countable things, *water, rice,* etc. (Similarly in English we should not normally add *s* to these nouns.) Other differences should be pursued in *Jamaican Creole Syntax* (Bailey, 1960), on which the above account draws. We should not forget either the considerable phonological differences between Creole and English.

How much Creole a West Indian immigrant possesses depends very much on such factors as the island he comes from, his social class, his urban or rural background. A person from a middle-class urban background will speak West Indian standard English, for instance. On the other hand, an un-educated speaker may switch from Creole to English and back in a single sentence, without being conscious of doing so. Thus the children of immigrants in the United Kingdom may have problems caused both by linguistic interference of Creole forms with British English, and by their confusion about the status of these forms.

2.4 IDIOLECT

The individual English speaker speaks a dialect of English. But he does not speak it exactly the same as everyone else. His pronunciation and voice quality are not the same as those of others; if they were, we should not be able to recognize people by their voices. But further, he makes a choice in lexis and grammar; he has his favourite words and constructions (some people never say *I think*, but *one would think*); he has favourite expressions and mannerisms, often unconscious; he speaks fast or slow, hesitates much or little; and so on. The term 'idiolect' has been coined to describe the speech habits of a single person.

2.5 REGISTER

So far we have been looking at language distinguished according to user. But there is the use to which he puts it in a particular situation. A variety distinguished according to use is called a 'register'. We shall develop this concept in the next chapter.

3. *LEVELS OF LANGUAGE*

The reader of this sentence is looking at two of the three elements which constitute it – its words (lexis), and the way they are arranged (its grammar). If he reads the sentence out aloud he will have supplied a third element – its phonology. It is common to call these the three 'levels' of language.

3.1 PHONOLOGY

The word 'phonology' is used to describe the sound system

of a language. We may think about the phonology of English from three aspects.

3.1.1 *Phonemes*, or individual sounds.

It is calculated that there are forty-four of these in English — vowels, diphthongs, and consonants. Actually, careful listening leads us to the discovery that there are many more: for instance, the *l* in *like* is not the same as the *l* in *well*. So that the forty-four phonemes are really families of sounds which are called 'allophones'. To a native speaker of English the difference between the pronunciation of the two *l*s is trivial; but to the native speaker of another language it might be as important as the distinction between *p* and *b* in *pit* and *bit*, giving a change of meaning. Native speakers cease to hear distinctions which are not significant for them; that is why, for instance, German speakers of English often pronounce *ws* as *vs*.

3.1.2 *Intonation*

Words are pronounced on a particular note (pitch) (pitch). 'Intonation' is the name given to the sequence of pitches that give the 'tune', sometimes called the 'intonation tune', of the sentence. Two very common tunes in English are those used for a statement and a question: Contrast the way the pitch gets lower in *we're going to go*, with the way it rises in *we're going to go?* An important point about pitch is that it is not an absolute, that is to say we don't always have to pronounce words on the same note to get the same meaning. A small girl with a treble voice and her father with a bass voice are obviously octaves apart, yet both are speaking English. What matters is the *contrast* between the tones: a tune played on the piano at different octaves, or in various keys, remains the same tune if the notes go up and down in the same relationship to one another on each occasion.

3.1.3 *Stress*

We give some syllables or words more emphasis than others; we stress them. We may distinguish two sorts of stress: that which is inseparable from the words, and that which we may vary. For instance, *military* has its main stress on the first syllable, and to emphasize the second (*lit*) would make near nonsense of it. Such a stress is inseparable from the word. And there are cases where nouns and verbs are distinguished by a change of stress: *export*, for instance. On the other hand, we can vary the stress in a sentence to produce different meanings. The reader may like to try the effect of stressing each word in turn in *I will go now*. The alternation of stressed and unstressed syllables produces rhythm. The words which receive stress tend to be nouns, verbs, adjectives, and adverbs; a fact which assumes some significance in language acquisition by young children. To this point we shall return.

3.2 LEXIS

The lexis of a language is its vocabulary, all those words which are in a dictionary. A word is the smallest unit that can function alone in a sentence, what Bloomfield (1935) calls 'a minimum free form'. It is not, however, necessarily the smallest unit of meaning: additions such as *un-, pre-, -ing, cran-* as in *cranberry*, are units of meaning. These, whether they are words or word elements, we call 'morphemes', a morpheme being the smallest unit of meaning. Morphemes which can occur alone, as a word, are called 'free', morphemes which cannot (e.g. *-ing*) are called 'bound'.

Let us confine ourselves to words at the moment, both singly and in combination. When we arrange words to make sentences we can use single words:

'The elephant dislikes his uncle.'

We can use common grammatical constructions.

'The elephant *will have been to see* his aunt.'

We can use collocations: that is, two or more words which commonly occur together:

'The elephant enjoys *eggs and bacon*.'
'The elephant *offers condolences to* his aunt.'

In these examples the italicized words operate as a single unit. Collocations, probable combinations of words, including idioms and metaphors, are far more common than is often realized, and we shall be developing this point later.

3·3   GRAMMAR

In a game like chess or draughts we have pieces, and we have rules for moving them. Thus the Bishop can only operate diagonally, the King can only move one square in any direction, and so on. In language the pieces are words, and we call the rules 'grammar'.

Basically there are two kinds of grammatical rules: those by which we arrange words in order; and those by which we make alterations to the form of, or add other words to, individual words. The first are rules of 'syntax', the 'orderly or systematic arrangement of parts or elements', as the *Oxford English Dictionary* puts it; the second are rules of 'accidence', including the making of 'inflections' or changes in the form of words.

The rules of syntax enable us to *order* words. *Bites dog man* is nonsense. There is only one likely order, *dog bites man*. We know that, in English, the subject usually precedes the verb, and this enables us to reject *man bites dog* (though it is syntactically correct); syntax tells us about position. Secondly, the rules tell us that we can only put certain kinds of words (parts of speech) next to others. We can say *a golden crown* (determiner, adjective, noun), but not *a golden is* (determiner, adjective, verb). Syntax tells us about co-occurrence. And thirdly, the rules guide us in deciding what we can replace in a sentence. In *dog bites man* we could replace *dog* by *the dog, the hungry dog,* but not by *the* or *hungry*). Syntax tells us about the possibilities of substitution.

The rules of accidence enable us to make changes in individual words. The main rules are:

1. Those enabling us to change to/from singular/plural in nouns: *elephant/elephants; child/children; man/men.*
2. Those enabling us to indicate possessives: the *child's book.*

3. Those indicating number and tense in verbs: *I walk/he walks; he was/will be/had been walking; he walked.*
4. Those enabling us to adjust the *case* of pronouns to be subjects, objects, or possessives: *I/me/my/mine.*
5. Those enabling us to change certain adjectives and adverbs to indicate degree: *good/better/best; small/smaller/smallest; beautiful, more/most beautiful.*

4. A SIMPLE GRAMMAR

'A grammar' is a description of a language that classifies its words by type, and states the rules for putting them together. The traditional grammatical system is known as 'formal grammar'; but of late years grammarians have pointed out its inadequacies, and have devised other systems. Anyone wanting an outline of some of these should consult Dixon (1965). The purpose of the following account is not to champion any one system, but to provide a terminology for use in the rest of this book.

4.1 WORD CLASSES

If we take a sentence like

'The *elephants* used to *give lovely flowers* to their *mothers formerly*,'

and we leave out the words underlined, we shall be left with

'The used to to their'.

If we leave out the other words we have

'Elephants give lovely flowers mothers formerly'.

It is quite clear which leaves us with most meaning. We should find it possible to supply the missing words with a fair chance of being right given the second, but given the first this would be quite impossible. We are thus led to perceive a distinction between two types of words – the one group contains those that carry most of the meaning, and the main function of the other is to relate these to one another. We therefore call the one group 'content words' or 'contentives', and the other group 'structure' or 'function words'. Some writers sum up the difference by describing the former as 'full', the latter as 'empty', words.

4.1.1 Content words

The traditional names of content words are noun (N), verb (V), adjective (A), and adverb (ADV). Fries (1963, p. 75) suggests that they may be recognized if they will fit one or more of three test frames:

A. The concert was good (always).

B. The clerk remembered the tax (suddenly).

C. A team went there.

Thus a noun is a word which will replace *concert, clerk, team*; a verb, *was, remembered, went*; an adjective, *good*; an adverb, *always, suddenly, there*; or one or more of them. It is only fair to add that Fries rejects the conventional terminology, and calls his classes, Class 1, 2, 3, and 4, for, using his frames, there will be both inclusions and exclusions from the traditional categories. Thus, if we tried to substitute a word like *father's* for *good* it would fit: *the concert was father's*, but it would not be an *adjective* in terms of traditional grammar. The use of the frame would, however, draw attention to its similarity to an adjective as used here. With these limitations in mind we can still find Fries's frames useful in discerning the traditional categories.

4.1.2 Structure words

We may classify the structure words as follows:

(a) *Determiners.* Words, occurring in the positions where *the* occurs, such as: the, a, these, those, some, my.

(b) *Modals and Auxiliaries*: may, might, should, would/to have, had, will have.

(c) *Negative*: not.

(d) *Intensifiers*: quite, really, fairly.

(e) *Conjunctions*: and, but, so.

(f) *Prepositions*: by, on, for, over.

(g) *Subordinatives*: after, because, if, until.

(i) *Personal pronouns*: I, me, mine, theirs.

One important difference between content words and structure words is that there are many thousands of the former (most of the language is made up of them); and only perhaps 200 of the latter, which are as a consequence used far more frequently. When we come to examine the topic of reading we shall see that fifteen structure words only make up a high percentage of the words used in reading matter.

4.2   BASIC SENTENCE PATTERNS

In order to make up sentences the content words and the structure words have to be arranged in some special order, according to certain rules of grammar. Some arrangements or patterns are much more common than others.

The basic sentence in English is one containing actor and action:

'The elephant eats.'
'The snail smiles.'

It often contains a recipient or consequence of the action:

'The elephant eats buns.'

The basic sentence has, in other words, two parts: subject and predicate. A subject always contains a noun or noun equivalent: for this reason we may call it a noun phrase (NP). A predicate always contains a verb or verb equivalent: for this reason we may call it a verb phrase (VP). Thus we may describe an English sentence (S):

$$S \rightarrow NP + VP$$

There are four basic patterns or 'kernel sentences', one involving the verb *to be* and the others involving the other verbs. In each sentence there are four basic word positions.

Pattern 1. A subject; verb (V) *to be* in any of its forms (was, will be, etc.); complement (noun or adjective), with optional adverb.

Pattern 2. A subject; intransitive verb, i.e. one not requiring an object to complete the sense (Vi); optional adverb.

NP	VP		
1	2	3	4
The elephant	is	a grandfather	(today)
The elephant	will be	hungry	(tomorrow)

Pattern 3. A subject; transitive verb, i.e. requiring an object (Vt); object; optional adverb.

NP	VP		
1	2	3	4
The zygodactyl	flies		(gracefully)
The brontosaurus	frightens the zygodactyl		(terribly)

Pattern 4. A subject; copulative verb (Vc); complement; optional adverb. A copulative verb is one of a comparatively small group (*look, seem, appear, become, feel*), functioning like *to be* in taking a complement (they are sometimes calling 'linking verbs').

NP	VP		
1	2	3	4
The brontosaurus	appears	angelic	(now)

4.3 DERIVED SENTENCES

In the previous section we have been using the terminology of Transformational Grammar, a way of looking at language associated with Noam Chomsky, whose *Syntactic Structures* (1957) and *Aspects of the Theory of Syntax* (1965) give technical presentations of the theory. Chomsky's work is difficult, but the basic idea of transformational grammar is very simple.

We have spoken of four types of kernel sentences. The theory is that one or other of these kernel sentences, or a combination of them, underlies all the sentences in the language

— sentences that are 'well-formed', that is, not fragments. We may 'derive' all other sentences from these kernel sentences; or to put it the other way, we may 'transform' the kernel sentence. Let us take:

'The brontosaurus frightens the zygodactyl.'

Expansion

'The *sensitive* brontosaurus *had* frightened the *modest* zygodactyl *unwittingly*.'

'The brontosaurus, *who was sensitive….*'

Interrogative

'*Does* the brontosaurus frighten the zygodactyl?'

'*Why does* the brontosaurus frighten the zygodactyl?'

'The brontosaurus frightens the zygodactyl, $\left.\begin{array}{l}\textit{doesn't he?}\\\textit{does he?}\end{array}\right.$'

Negative

'The brontosaurus *does not* frighten the zygodactyl.'

Passive

'The zygodactyl *is* frightened *by* the brontosaurus.'

Completely new words are printed in italics, but transformations may require other modifications of existing words: for instance, in the first Interrogative example the *s* disappears from the verb 'frighten' with the introduction of 'Does'. The original sentence kernels show the 'deep structure' of the sentence, the form of words shows its 'surface structure'.

The transformationalists do not argue that we go through a process of transformation every time we utter a sentence; though, as we shall see, it seems that a young child does learn very simple patterns, and is helped to build them up, transform them, by adults surrounding him. Primarily, however, transformational grammar is a way of describing language, a way of classification, which points out to us, enables us to discuss, certain of its qualities.

5. *THE USE OF GRAMMAR*

Systems of grammar are means of describing the language; they give us insight into each feature and working and enable us to talk about it. As we have said, there are various systems of grammar available at the moment. The structural grammar associated with the name of Fries is described in his *The Structure of English* (1963). A useful popularization is that by Newsome (1962). This was influential in the fifties, particularly in the U.S.A., but the weight of attention switched in the sixties to Transformational Grammar, best approached through the expositions of Thomas (1965) and Roberts (1962). Transformational Grammar is concerned with the 'well-formed sentence'. An approach which might eventually be more comprehensively descriptive is that of the 'Edinburgh' linguists: *Scale and Category Grammar*, Halliday, 1962; Halliday *et al.*, 1964; Sinclair, 1971. The theory is still evolving, but Berry (1971) gives the simplest account available. Perhaps the best introduction to the grammar of modern English, not tied to any particular theory, is that by Mittins (1962).

5.1 RESEARCH ON FORMAL GRAMMAR

It is, however, important for us to be quite clear what the use of grammar is. It is useful as a descriptive and analytical tool, as we have said. But the other claims made for it are nearly all completely without foundation, as has been demonstrated by massive research over seventy years. The researches are carried out with traditional grammar, but there is no reason to think their findings would be different with other systems.

As early as 1903 the pioneer American research worker J. M. Rice made an extensive study, which strongly suggested that the learning of formal grammar had no beneficial effect on children's written work; and by 1929, when R. L. Lyman brought out his *Summary of Investigations*, it was only possible to assert a beneficial effect through ignorance (or defiance) of the evidence of a large number of empirical studies. Since then researches have multiplied still more; and the results have been the same. They are here summarized, and a few of the many studies instanced.

(i) *Training in formal grammar does not improve pupils' composition.* Asker found a very low correlation between ability in composition and proficiency in grammar amongst students at Washington University (1923). Macaulay obtained similar results with Scottish children (1947). A study (1960) by Robinson compared children's scores on general ability, parts of speech recognition, and sentence analysis, with their gradings on three compositions; and it found little relationship between the scores on grammar and the grades on composition.

(ii) *Ability in grammar is more related to that in some other subjects than to that in English composition.* Boraas (1917) found higher correlations between scores in grammar and those in history, geography, and arithmetic than between those in grammar and those in composition. Segal and Barr (1926) found this relationship was no more than that between the members of any other pair of normal school subjects.

(iii) *A knowledge of grammar is of no general help in correcting faulty usage.* Catherwood (1932) asked school children to correct sentences each containing one item of faulty usage, and to give reasons. Good scores were obtained on correction; but poor ones on the grammatical rules explaining them. Benfer (1935) also found a low relationship between a knowledge of grammar and an ability to correct sentences, even though he made a special effort to teach the application of grammatical principles.

(iv) *Grammar is often taught to children who have not the maturity or intelligence to understand it.* Macaulay found in a survey of 1,000 children in Glasgow (1947) that the average pupil of twelve can recognize only common nouns and simple verbs, despite training. At the end of a three-year secondary school course only 41·5 per cent of pupils were able to score

50 per cent on the five simple parts of speech. He concluded that formal grammar should not be taught to pupils under fourteen; after that they are more able to grasp its concepts. Symonds (1931) demonstrated that the ability to make any use of grammatical concepts in real language situations is confined to very bright children.

(v) *Grammar and foreign language learning.* Pressey and Robinson (1944) concluded that a knowledge of grammar is helpful – *if* the language is approached through grammatical categories. There is no evidence that grammar is helpful to direct method learning.

(vi) *Does grammar hinder the development of children's English?* The implication of many studies is not only that the teaching of grammar does not help children's written English, but that it may hinder it. The main reason is that the amount of time spent on grammar may be at the expense of other things (Macaulay, 1947); but there are indications that it may also introduce confusions. Sears and Diebel (1916) found that eighth-grade pupils who had received instruction in formal grammar made more mistakes in using pronouns than third-grade pupils who had received no such instruction.

(viii) *Does written work suffer if grammar is dispensed with?* Heath (1962) based the work of one group of pupils on 'library-centred English', without formal exercises of any kind; and the work of another on 'classroom English', including normal exercises in grammar. After nine months the first group were significantly ahead in their composition work, without loss of accuracy. An earlier experiment by Bagley (1937) showed that boys who studied literature for thirty-three weeks wrote better and more accurate compositions after that time than boys who studied only grammar.

It should be noted that the above research has been carried out with Traditional Grammar. However, it seems unlikely that the results would prove different with any of the new grammars. They depend on the essential differences between an analytical categorizing activity and a synthesizing specific activity rather than on the merits of any particular system.

6. SUMMARY

Each English-speaking person speaks an idiolect and a choice of registers (depending on the situation) that are forms of a dialect; this, in turn, is a form of the English language, which is one of the family of languages known as Indo-European.

We think of language as having three levels – of sound (phonology), of words (lexis), and of structure (grammar).

When talking about language we need a terminology in which to describe it, and we call this terminology 'a grammar'. There are various grammars, and a simple 'transformational grammar' has been described.

However, 'grammar' is a descriptive instrument, and not basically a means of developing one's own speech and writing. This statement can be supported by massive research, a few examples of which are referred to.

CHAPTER II

LANGUAGE AND SITUATION

1. *THE COMMUNICATIONS SITUATION*

1.1 CONTEXT OF SITUATION

We have so far written about language in general. But it is, of course, clear that no language can exist outside a situation – even sentences quoted as examples in a book of this kind are in the situation of being in a book, and are determined by the points the author wishes to make. But that might be called an artificial situation; nearly all other language occurs in natural situations. And the situation has a considerable effect on the language. Malinowski was dissatisfied with the way scholars confined themselves to the study of texts and of verbal context; he felt that what he called the 'context of situation' should be taken into account:

exactly as a single word is – save in exceptional circumstances – meaningless, and receives its significance only through the context of other words, so a sentence usually appears in the context of other sentences and has meaning only as part of a larger significant whole. I think it is very **profitable** in linguistics to widen the concept of context so that it embraces not only the spoken words but facial expression, gesture, bodily activities, the whole group of people present during an exchange of utterances and the part of the environment on which these people are engaged (quoted in Dixon, 1965, p. 88).

Let us take this wider view then, and look, not simply at the language alone, but at the elements in a 'communication situation' which produce it. To do so we will devise a communications 'model': the term 'model' used in this sense means a simplification bringing out the essential elements, which can thus refer not only to one situation but to many.

1.2 A COMMUNICATIONS MODEL

Let us imagine an elevator. A man gets in; there is a woman already there. The elevator moves up. The man says nothing to the woman; he does not look at her, certainly he does not look her in the eyes (which in British society is almost equivalent to assault). Then the elevator gets stuck between floors. The man feels prompted to speak (he may feel prompted to scream, but controls himself). He says something like 'Not to worry: they'll soon fix it.' The woman says, perhaps, 'Yes.' And so on. Here we have a person to speak, a person to listen, a subject in common, and a context; we have the four principal elements in a 'communications situation': an Addressor (the man), an Addressee (the woman to whom he speaks), a Subject (the jammed elevator), and a Context or environment (the elevator which is their prison). The unfortunate couple have in fact conveniently provided for us a communications model. Let us draw this as follows:

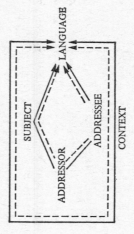

The language which comes out arises from the contributions of the various elements, and will vary from situation to situation. In the model the continuous and the dotted lines are meant to indicate that a particular element may play a major or minor part. Let us consider their contributions.

The Addressor will speak an idiolect of English, and a dialect of English. The words he chooses will be governed by his intentions, which will of course be strictly honourable. In other circumstances his intentions might be to instruct, to disprove, to persuade, to seduce. Here they are: First, to establish contact – this use of language we call 'phatic communion' (greetings and small talk, subjects like health, the weather, the price of things, are examples). Second, he is concerned to reassure (both the woman and himself), rather than to do other things, like communicating information (of which he has very little – he probably doesn't *know* whether they'll soon repair the elevator). In contrast, were he an elevator engineer he would probably reassure the woman in the same way, but his language would be different. He might do it by explaining, in non-technical language, what was wrong.

The Addressee also influences the language used. Men often speak to women in a way different from that they use with other men. An example of this is the comparative absence of swearing; other differences may be matters of vocabulary, maybe in the choice of subjects men think women like or are able to discuss. More subtle is the general tone often adopted – anything from high medieval chivalry to low modern chattuppery. But the Addressee contributes to the language of the Addressor also by response. Had the woman in the elevator replied 'Oh I hope so, I'm frightened,' the man's next sentence would not be the same as if she had said 'I don't speak to strange men in elevators.'

The Subject (sometimes called 'Referent', what is referred to) obviously supplies a good deal of the language. After all, we are in great difficulty talking about the situation under discussion if we can't use words like 'elevator'). Had the two people in the elevator been elevator engineers, then they might have discussed, in a technical vocabulary, what was wrong, and the language would have been different. As it is, the man does not know the technical vocabulary.

The Context is the elevator and the atmosphere of crisis within it. This might affect the language in various ways. For one thing, the physical setting makes it unnecessary to use words about certain things; we do not speak about present objects in the way we do about absent ones. The man might say 'Try pressing that', without needing to say 'Try pressing the top button on the control panel.' For another thing, the crisis atmosphere will help to produce urgent rather than deliberate, emotional rather than rational, speech. Contrast a pub, where the relaxed atmosphere might encourage informal casual speech. Malinowski would include also under 'context of situation' all those other means of communication – a look, a gesture, a touch of reassurance – which affect the language, in that they replace or supplement it. (The model is taken from Wilkinson, 1968.)

2. REGISTER

The kind or 'variety' of English appropriate for a particular purpose in a particular situation (that is, having regard to Subject, Addressee, and Context) is known as a 'register' of English. A register can, of course, be either in the spoken or written language. There are many spoken registers, and there are many written registers.

Differences between registers are partly a matter of lexis: a wrestling commentator would use 'forearm smash' and 'pile driver', a priest 'grace', 'conversion', 'divinity'. They are partly a matter of grammar; the sentences of the priest will probably be longer and more complex than those of the commentator. The construction will differ. Thus a cookery book will leave out personal words like 'I' and 'you', and be as economical as possible: 'Mix well together and leave until quite cold.' A science text-book will be impersonal in another way, using the passive voice: 'The calx is heated to redness.' A poet would be likely to be more personal and use words to bring out their feeling. 'My love is like a red, red rose.' And, of course, where registers are *spoken* there is the question of phonology to be considered. A news-reader has a delivery different from those of a disc-jockey, a judge, a priest, or a school-teacher talking to infants.

Various sub-divisions of register have been suggested, and

various terms for them have been proposed. The terminology is sometimes contradictory, or at least confusing (for an examination of terms see Gregory, 1967). Readers who want to pursue the subject should consult Strang (1962), Halliday, McIntosh, and Strevens (1964), Spencer and Gregory (1964), and particularly Strevens (1965, Ch. 6). The following attempts to give a simple exposition of the main issues.

If we reflect on the communications model above, we can, as it were, bisect it by horizontal line; we can see that the language of the Addressor might be influenced more by the Subject, or more by the Addressee, and that this influence will vary from circumstance to circumstance. This fact provides us with two convenient divisions of register for *the purpose of analysis* (in usage there are often no such clear-cut distinctions). These two are Addressor-Subject registers, and Addressor-Addressee registers.

2.1 ADDRESSOR-SUBJECT REGISTERS

These are registers in which the Addressor is concentrating on the exposition or communication of the Subject. Thus the language of trades, professions, games – technical terms, 'jargon' – would come into this class. In these circumstances there tends to be considerable knowledge shared with the Addressee:

When the mixture is ignited, the products of combustion expand down the cylinder which is fitted with a reciprocating piston. The downward movement of the piston is converted into a rotational movement of the crankshaft by means of a connecting rod.

(Herbert, 1965, p. 66.)

Allowing for the Franciscan religious (in the technical sense) divergencies and for the personal theological emphasis we must still call the mediaeval philosopher Duns Scotus Augustinian in that he retained the most fundamental epistemological doctrines of the received Augustinian tradition, the knowability of the individual, the primacy of will, and his concern for the argument of St. Anselm.

(A broadcast sermon.)

He was caught in the leg-trap off a googlie from Smith who thus completed his hat trick.

(The game of cricket.)

Some subject-focused registers are mainly written, because in writing the Addressor is less concerned with immediate contact with, and understanding by, the Addressee. If the Addressee fails to understand the first time he can always read the passage again. A notable example of this is in the field of law, where the special language used for acts, statutes, and other legal documents uses exact and traditional terminology and sentence structure, not at all so as to communicate immediately, but so as to avoid ambiguity in interpretation by lawyers trained in interpretation. The *spoken* language of lawyers, even when arguing a legal point, is not so dense and involved, otherwise they would not understand one another. And of course they do not begin each sentence with *Whereas*.

2.2 ADDRESSOR-ADDRESSEE REGISTERS

At the other pole there are the registers which focus on the Addressee. (These are sometimes classed as 'style' or 'tenor' of speaking.) They will be the registers of social life, where the intention is less merely to communicate information, more to establish and maintain social relationships. These relationships will be in the family, with friends, with colleagues at work, strangers in the street; between young and old, people of superior and inferior status, employer and employee, and so on. At the one end there will be 'phatic communion' – the interchange of pleasantries about the weather, prices, or other general topics; at the other there may be the deep personal involvement and self-analysis of a couple in love, or a psychiatrist and his patient.

There, there, that's a good boy. Bye-bye now. How's mummy's little boy now? Better? That's right. Bye-bye. Mummy's got to go and get daddy's supper. She'll come if you want her. Shh. Bye-bye now.

You shall nowe receive (my deare wife) my last words, in these my last lines, my Love I send you that you may keepe itt, when I am dead, and my Counsell that you may remember itt, when I am noe more; I would not by my will present you with Sorrowes (Dear Besse) Lett them goe into the grave with mee; and be buried in the dust, And seeing itt is not the will of God, that I shall see you any more in this life, beare itt patiently, and with an heart like thy selfe.

(Walter Raleigh to his wife.)

A. Nice to see you had a good journey.
B. All right till ' got to Birmingham/then that central ring.
A. Yes, most confusing isn't it?

Addressee-focused registers are more likely to be spoken than written. When they are written it is often because the Addressee is envisaged as an individual, as in personal letter-writing (Raleigh, for example). In such letters people probably come nearest to recording their own speech.

Differences between such registers in the spoken mode are often a matter of tone; one is not so matey with the college principal as with one's room-mate. But they are also a matter of the lexis and grammar. A man phones three people:

A. Of course. I'll go round and see Mr. Harris straight away. I'll report to you personally as soon as I know. Good afternoon.

B. Not at all. It'll be a pleasure. Let you know as soon as I've got it fixed with Davies. What's the address? O.K. Cheerio!

C. Well, I could step in on the way home. Means I'd be a bit late though. What's the address? You're quite sure that's where he lives? Right. Bye for now.

'A' is spoken to his employer, 'B' to his friend, and 'C' to his wife. 'A', spoken to the friend or the wife, would have sounded too formal. 'C', to the wife, is not grudging; he is in fact considering her, realizing the dinner will have gone cold if he is late, and asking whether she is prepared for this. He can question whether she's got the right address without seeming critical. But if he used the same words to the employer they would seem both grudging and critical. 'B' to the friend is less formal in language than 'A', and contains the phrase 'It'll be a pleasure.' He would not use this to his employer, as it would sound as if he were doing his job as a special favour: he would not use it to his wife, as favours are out of place between husband and wife – their marriage is a joint enterprise, in which, in one sense, they are always doing favours for each other, but neither thinks of their contributions in this way. 'A' to the employer, is much more formal and less personal than the other two. If the speaker has any doubts about the address of Mr. Harris, he keeps them to himself; he can always check with the secretary. A phrase like 'report to you' implies an employer/employee relationship.

In the above examples the mode of address has been left out, as it is a clear indicator of relationship. Brown and Ford (1964) carried out an interesting survey of American English usage in business. They found the two principal modes of address were the first name (*John*), and the last name with a title (*Mr. Smith*). Address by last name alone they did not find common; in the U.K. it would seem to be more in use, both in the Civil Service, and by teachers to schoolboys, but not schoolgirls. Brown and Ford distinguish three usages: the reciprocal exchange of first names; the reciprocal exchange of title and last name; and the non-reciprocal pattern, where one uses the first name, and the other the title and last name. There appears to be more preference for title and last name among older colleagues of equal status than among younger, who use first names after a slight acquaintance. Employers may call their more distant subordinates by first name, but will expect title and last name in return. Subordinates closer in status to their employer may use his first name, may in fact over-use it, to demonstrate intimacy; subordinates not quite able to use the first name will often not use the title and surname either, but use *you*. Kinship, age, sex, occupation, origins, amount of contact, status, all have some influence. The study was carried out predominantly in the U.S.A As has been hinted, there would probably be some interesting comparison to be made with the U.K.

2·3   LANGUAGE STYLES

The work of Joos (1961) draws our attention to certain aspects of the Addressor-Addressee relationship; how, for instance, the age, 'gentility', and 'sense of responsibility' of the participants affect the language. In particular, he writes of five 'styles' of language; that is to say how the language takes into account the closeness or distance between the participants:

Frozen. A style for writing. It is frozen in the sense that it is not subject to change by interaction with the Addressee, and so permanent – it may become 'literature'.

Formal. A style of pre-involvement, a style in which, for instance, introductions take place. It has formal phrases ('May I introduce . . .') in which the Addressor is not committing himself to more than a distant relationship.

Consultative. The style for coming to terms with strangers. The Addressor supplies background information – not assuming he will be understood without it; and the Addressee participates continuously. This is the norm for most conversation.

Casual. Insiders, people within a particular social group – friends, colleagues, acquaintances – don't have to supply information to one another in the way they do to strangers. The casual style is marked by ellipsis (omission) of words, syllables. 'Can I help you?' is consultative. 'C'n I help you?' is casual. It is also marked by slang.

Intimate. Usually between two people, between whom so much information is shared that what Joos called 'jargon' is used (i.e. words with a special meaning for the two (see 2.4 below)), and parts of sentences only may be employed, what he calls 'Extraction' (e.g. 'Ready?' for 'Are you ready?' In this pronunciation of 'Ready?' even the question intonation may have disappeared also).

2.4 REGISTER AND SHARED KNOWLEDGE

We have already mentioned the influence of Context on language. If, for instance, objects are present they can just be referred to or pointed to – they don't have to be described. In the same way, people who live together in the same house, community, or place of work, have a good deal in common that doesn't need to be put into words at great length. Thus the language they do use one to another carries much more meaning than it does to an outsider. It may even be abbreviated. Interesting examples of such uses of language occur in families which have their own words, jokes, stock of knowledge.

Let us take an imaginary conversation between a husband and wife at the tea-table.

WIFE: Saw Mrs. Edwards in Walker's.
HUSBAND: Buying a pith helmet?
WIFE: They didn't have Danish Blue.
HUSBAND: Where's the soap then?
WIFE: I think Tom's all right really.
HUSBAND: House far too big for one thing.

To understand this we need to know that Mr. and Mrs. Edwards have come to live in the neighbourhood, and have bought a house which the husband in our conversation thinks is too grand for them. The Edwards have spent some years in the East and can talk of little else. As a result, the husband finds Mr. Edwards pompous and thinks it a pity he doesn't go abroad for good – hence his remark about buying a pith helmet. The wife, however, is quite impressed with Mr. Edwards, 'Tom,' as she calls him. We can guess that Walker's is the grocer's – despite the husband's remark about the pith helmet – where the wife is buying cheese. We need one more piece of information – that the family's name for processed cheese – what some people call 'mousetrap' – is 'soap'. If we have these pieces of information, if we know what meaning attaches to particular words or phrases in this family, then we have no difficulty in following the conversation. The husband

and wife do not use a large number of words, as they would
have had to if they were making the conversation clear to
strangers. Their sentences are very economical, but the words
they *do* use are full of meaning.

It is when we come to speak outside such restricted situations that rather more difficulty arises. There may be several
reasons for this, and one is that we may need to use other
words to explain our meaning. In giving directions we could
say to a member of our own family: 'Just near where the old
police station was', and be sure of being understood. But a
stranger to the town would not have this information, and we
should have to make an effort of imagination to see how the
landscape would look to him: 'Just beyond the demolition
site, the one where they're using the tower crane.' And to
explain, we should need more words than with the first direction. We often fail to explain as well as we might because we
do not realize how restricted is the meaning of some of the
words we use to other people.

Of course the language the married couple use to each other
is communicating very effectively in that situation: but it
could not be used generally—it is 'restricted'). A similar situation arises when we come to consider the language of some
people with little education; in their own families and amongst
their own friends they can make their needs and desires
known, say what they want to say at a level which the others
will understand. But once outside these situations they are
restricted; they are described as speaking a 'restricted code'.
To put it another way, they have only one register—that of
the home, or street, or playground. When they have to use
language outside these situations they lack the ability to
verbalize that comes from speaking beyond things immediately present, or about which people know already. This is a
matter we shall return to in a later chapter.

3. SPOKEN AND WRITTEN ENGLISH

The invention of the recorder has made it possible for us

to catch and study speech of all sorts in a way that we were never able to do before. And we find that spoken English is often quite a long way removed from written English. It is not better or worse – but different, because doing a different job. We sometimes say, by way of intended compliment, that someone 'speaks like a book', but as a matter of fact anybody who did this would on most occasions sound intolerably formal and stilted.

To bring out some of the differences between the spoken and the written language let us examine the transcription of a recording of a speaker on a fairly informal occasion (the speaker concerned was relaxing over a cup of coffee with colleagues).

he was as it were/you know him do you/how shall I say/er *withdrawn*/er/shut-in/*as though he had a kind of*/mm/*goldfish bowl round his head*/not very easy.

The words in italics form the sentence as it would probably be if we were writing it. All the other words are in some sense characteristic of spoken rather than written English.

There is a freer form of sentences in the spoken language. This group of words has two other sentences stuck in the middle of it ('you know him do you' and 'how shall I say'). In the spoken language we are much more tolerant towards the form of our sentences than in the written language. We often pause, not where we should in writing, and run on from the middle of one sentence to the middle of the next, if the words seem to belong together. Despite what school books tell us about a sentence having a main verb, many of our spoken word groups have no verb at all (as with the finishing words 'not very easy' in the transcription).

The spoken language is characterized by greater *re-dundancy*. In industry this word is used when there are too many workers for the jobs available. In discussing the *written* language we apply it when more words than are strictly necessary are used to do the job of communication; it is regarded as a fault. In the *spoken* language, however, it need not be a fault at all but a positive virtue. If we are reading and we do not wholly grasp the meaning, we can read the troublesome sentences again. But we cannot look over speech in this way – it has gone, and gone swiftly. The speaker needs to make sure his important points are grasped first time. The communication systems used in the Forces and elsewhere realize the difference between a spoken and a written message. The printed message coming through on ticker-tape might read: 'Return to base'; if it were coming over by speech on RT it would contain repetition: 'Return to base, I say again, return to base.'

This repetition, or redundancy, is not usually made completely consciously. In the 'goldfish bowl' transcription the speaker is telling his listeners, no less than three times, of the difficulty his acquaintance has in making contact with people. He tells us he is 'withdrawn', 'shut-in', and that it is 'as though he had a goldfish bowl round his head'. He does not say to himself 'I'll put it in three different ways', but his concern with making his point effectively leads him to do so.

The spoken language contains 'echo-sounding' devices. When the speaker says of the man, in the midst of his account, 'you know him do you?', he is seeking a sign that his listener is with him. He is also drawing the listener in. A speaker before an audience is gaining all kinds of responses from them which are signals back in answer to his usually unspoken question: 'Are you receiving me?' These signals might be looks of boredom, puzzlement, or pleasure; frowns, yawns, or nods; laughter; or murmurs of approval or disapproval. In conversation the signals will range from expression and gesture, through grunts and words like 'mm' and 'yes', to answers to questions, comments, and contributions to the subject under discussion. In this way the listener influences very much what the speaker is saying. If the speaker receives signals of puzzlement he will probably increase the degree of redundancy in his speech, so as to make his point clear. Particularly in conversation, many of us find a completely silent, expressionless listener very disconcerting; we expect him to contribute. By his signals he can change completely the course of the conversation – by introducing a different topic, for instance. Speech in conversation or discussion is a two-way process; the participants are mutually dependent and we call this characteristic of speech 'reciprocity'.

Another characteristic of the spoken language in the transcription is its 'stabilizers'. This is the term we give to pauses, hesitations, and words like 'er' and 'mm'. These used to be thought faults, and children were often told not to say 'er'. We are now realizing that to 'er' is human. Stabilizers such as this occur particularly when we are thinking aloud, defining more precisely, seeking a vivid expression, as the speaker is in the transcription. They help the listener also by pacing the ideas and helping him to think with the speaker. To some extent phrases like 'kind of' and 'sort of' fulfil a similar function; they often precede a metaphor which the speaker would be shy of without some lead-in. They are often springboards to creative expression. Normally we do not notice stabilizers; it is only when they are obtrusive, are indeed a sign, not of more creative expression, but that expression is breaking down, that they are to be condemned. 'He was you know, er, kind of, mm, sort of, er, you know . . .', for instance contains far too many stabilizers. In a case like this, one might call them 'fillers'.

As we have seen, there are various registers of the spoken language. The English of the transcription would be too informal for a judge's summing-up in a court of law, where a considered, deliberate utterance is required. A public oration at a university would be very formal indeed, closely resembling *written* English, and so would some sermons, though there is a tendency today for the parson to deliver a 'talk' rather than an 'address'. Everyday conversation tends to be fairly informal, and characterized by some of the features we have noted. It is the type of speech we use most of the time.

4. CORRECT ENGLISH

Two boys are fighting in the school playground. One manages to pin down the other, who mutters through clenched teeth: 'Gerroutovit Holmesy, I'll fill yer in, honest I will.' A schoolmaster approaches, and the two boys rise shamefacedly. The master says he will not have that sort of thing going on, and tells the victim that what he should have said was: 'If you do not get off my chest, Holmes, I will not be answerable for the consequences.' He thinks he is advising the boy on correct English, but what he suggests is actually incorrect in a very real sense. It would not work; indeed it would be greeted with derision. *In the circumstances* the schoolmaster's suggestion is *bad* English, not because it is ungrammatical (it is perfectly in order grammatically) but because it is *inappropriate*.

That there is one absolute 'correct English' is a doctrine that still lurks behind many vehement but uninformed debates on language. Nowadays we recognize that we cannot judge the 'correctness' of an utterance without taking account of the situation in which it is used. Yet the doctrine has a long history: it was formulated with great clarity in the Augustan period, when men paid a good deal of attention to the rules of language. There is a passage in the Preface to Johnson's great *Dictionary* (1755) in which he speaks of the principles which have guided his choice of words:

That many terms of art and manufacture are omitted must be frankly acknowledged; but for this defect I may boldly allege that it was unavoidable; I could not visit caverns to learn the miner's language, nor take a voyage to perfect my skill in the dialect of navigation, nor visit the warehouses of merchants, and shops of artificers, to gain the name of wares, tools and operations, of which no mention is found in books; what favourable accident or easy enquiry brought within my reach, has not been neglected, but it had been a hopeless labour to glean up words by courting living information, and contesting with the sullenness of one, and the roughness of another.

The 'terms of art and manufacture', 'miner's language', and 'dialect of navigation' are what we should nowadays call registers of the spoken language. Johnson could not, of course, 'court living information' — these registers — as easily as we can with tape-recorders — nor would he have wanted to.

Such words did not really interest him, they would probably be 'sullen', 'rough', 'low', 'bad', or 'barbarous', to quote a few of the terms of disapprobation in his dictionary. Their chief fault was that they were words 'of which no mention is found in books'. For Johnson the written language was the norm, the 'correct' usage. Now we prefer to speak of 'appropriateness' of language. For the various roles we play in society we acquire various languages or codes – what J. R. Firth (1959) calls 'being in command of a constellation of restricted languages, satellite languages so to speak, governed by personality in social life, and the general language of the community'.

Is it then no longer possible to speak of 'incorrect' or 'bad' English? Certainly we may do so, but on rather different grounds. The grounds are (i) effectiveness of communication, and (ii) acceptability. Thus 'we didn't ought to have ate it' succeeds on the first ground (there is no doubt what the speaker means), but fails on the second (it would not be acceptable to the international community of educated users of the language). As for the first, it applies in the three levels of language: phonology, lexis, and grammar. If the speaker's accent or pronunciation is very different from the norm, for regional or class dialect reasons, or through speech defect, so that he is not understood by the majority; if his lexis is misused (Mrs. Malaprop in Sheridan's *Rivals* spoke of 'an allegory on the banks of the Nile'); or if his grammar is deviant, we might call his English 'bad English'. The second, suitability in situation, we have already illustrated. Here 'bad' English would be the kind the schoolmaster advised in the illustration, at the beginning of this section, for use in the playground. But effectiveness and acceptability often go together. A chairman who addresses a member of a committee 'You great steaming nit; shut up if you can't talk sense!' communicates his meaning; but his language is unacceptable, and because it is unacceptable it may well fail in its intention of silencing his opponent. It may be counter-productive. (Useful papers on 'correctness' are Mittins, 1969, and Warburg, 1962.)

5. *SUMMARY*

Language does not exist outside a situation of some kind, which influences it. We have looked (in terms of a communications model) at the elements in this situation – the person speaking (Addressor), the burden of what he is saying (Subject), the person to whom he is speaking (Addressee), and the place, occasion, etc. (Context) in which he is speaking. The language which is the outcome of the interaction between these elements we call a 'register'.

Register may be regarded for convenience as being more Subject-oriented or more Addressee-oriented (the language of an encyclopedia is different from the language of love, for example). Registers are both spoken and written; and between spoken and written English there may be marked differences depending on the situation.

We judge a register according to its effectiveness as communication and its suitability to a particular situation. Thus we no longer think, as did people formerly, of *one* 'correct English', but of many correct Englishes; we think of 'appropriateness' rather than 'correctness'.

CHAPTER III

THE ACQUISITION OF LANGUAGE

1. *THE BEGINNINGS OF LANGUAGE*

1.1 THE FIRST NOISES

Take one baby. Consider his first noises. Louise Macneice represents an unborn child as uttering a 'Prayer Before Birth'. Although there is some evidence that a five-months-old foetus may make noises of a kind (McCarthy, 1954), it is intrinsically unlikely that he would speak a poem of eight stanzas, which in any case would be difficult to record. We must content ourselves with the noises he makes after birth.

The first cry the baby makes is his response to the shock of birth as he draws his first breath. In the next weeks his cries become differentiated into what Lewis (who shows they can be distinguished phonetically) calls 'comfort and discomfort noises' (1963), which every mother can recognize from about the fourth month, whatever others think of them. The baby will react to noise, but soon learns to select the human voice for attention, particularly that of his mother, since it is often accompanied by the warmth and security of bodily contact and by nourishment. He will be seen listening to conversations going on in the room.

1.2 BABBLING

The baby's early noises become syllabic, and repetitive. They are known as 'babble'. He seems to babble for the sheer enjoyment of it. But it serves other functions also. He is, for instance, practising articulation. The most noticeable function, however, is the production of sounds which adults shape into words. Obviously he will make the sounds he finds easiest, and this accounts for the predominance of noises which we represent by *ma-ma-ma, da-da-da*, and so on. Work is going on on the order of acquisition of acceptable sounds (reported, for instance, in Ingram, 1969). The parents seize on the sounds which approximate to the words they want to teach – *Mama, Daddy*, etc. – and encourage them, often by imitating the baby's babble as exactly as they can – *ma-ma, da-da*. Thus they separate them out from the stream of noises the baby produces. It was formerly supposed that all the sounds of all the languages of the world were to be found in this stream of noises, and that the parents reinforced some and extinguished others in accordance with the requirements of their own language, but this is not the case. All children seem to have a certain range of sounds in common, but from Irwin's work it appears that other sounds peculiar to individual languages have to be learnt from the adults speaking them (McCarthy, 1954).

In language throughout the world, therefore, because they are based on sounds which babies produce early, the first words tend to have a correspondence. Lewis speaks of 'six archetypal nursery words' – *mama, nana, papa, baba, tata, dada* (1963, p. 33). Thus English has *mama*, French *maman*, German *mama*, Italian *mamma*, Swahili *mama*, and Chinese *mah*. But the sounds are not always given the same meaning by adults. In Georgian, one of the languages spoken in South Russia, *mama* perversely stands for *father*, and *dada* for *mother*; in Swahili *baba* is *father*. These illustrate well the customary definition of language as an arbitrary system of vocal symbols by which a speech community co-operates.

Babble may be said to serve three purposes: enjoyment, equivalent to play; the practice of skill in making sounds; and the provision of a stream of sounds from which parents select in helping to equip the baby with his first words.

1.3   FIRST LANGUAGE

When parents detect the baby's first words they claim that he is beginning to talk. And this is true, in that without first words there will never be further words. But to the linguist single words do not constitute language, which depends on the relationship of one word to another. These single words are now known as 'holophrases'. They are developments of the comfort and discomfort noises made earlier. In many ways they correspond to the different noises animals make. A baby cries *mama* and this may 'mean' 'I am in distress: rescue me.' A dog whines at the door and this 'means' 'I want to go out'; he growls and this 'means' 'Come one step nearer, mate, and I'll have your throat out'. But neither dog nor baby is capable of formulating his meaning linguistically in the way we have just done.

The normal child at about a year old will say simple words. In the next six or twelve months he will make 'sentences' of two or three words. It is convenient to use the term 'sentence' for these early groups of words, but, as we shall see, they do not necessarily correspond to adult sentences. By the age of three-and-a-half or four the child will be in possession of the essential structures of the language. What this means we shall be in a better position to understand later on, when we come to examine transcriptions of the spoken language of children of that age (see Chapters VI, 4 and VII, 2.3 below). The miraculous acquisition of language in so short a time is often commented upon. We have to remember, however, that it is practically a full-time occupation for the child over a period of three years, which represent a very large number of language-learning hours.

2. *THE LANGUAGE-ACQUISITION DEVICE*

Language is acquired by imitation, but not only by imitation.

There is normally immense motivation in the child to be like his parents – they so huge, he so tiny and insignificant. And thus he will imitate them, particularly his mother, because he spends most time with her, and imitates her speech.

From adults and other children he gains his vocabulary by imitation; he has no other means of gaining it. His whole mental dictionary, all the words he uses, will be built up in this way.

A dictionary is, however, of very little use if one does not know how to arrange the words it contains. The use of language lies in the arrangement of words one has acquired. The use of language *cake eat*, *Eat daddy cake*, *Eat cake daddy* are unacceptable attempts at *Daddy eat cake*, though not so unacceptable as *Cake eat daddy*. The correct arrangement can be acquired by imitation. If the child hears *Daddy eat(s) cake* he will be able to repeat it, and use it when appropriate. So far, then, imitation provides a perfectly adequate explanation of the child's language acquisition.

The difficulty comes when the child utters sentences he can never have heard. One can easily envisage a situation where he sees for the first time a dog given a biscuit, and says *Dog eat bikky*. He is not imitating here; there are no dogs at his house, and anyway his parents would not approve of their being fed with biscuits, so he can never have heard the sentence spoken. What he has acquired is the underlying subject-verb-object pattern from hearing *Daddy eat(s) cake*, and many other sentences like it. He has, we say, 'abstracted' this pattern, and can arrange other words in it as he requires. But this pattern is capable of many variations in itself:

> 'Daddy is/was/will be eating cake.'
> 'Daddy is not eating cake.'
> 'Will daddy eat cake?'
> 'Where is daddy eating cake?'

These variations are called 'transformations' of the basic sentence pattern. Just as the child does not have to hear all possible basic sentences to be able to use them, so he does not have to hear all possible transformations to use them. He learns the rules for making them. It is often learnt early that to make negatives one adds *not*: *Daddy not eat cake*; but this rule is, of course, incomplete – one needs also to transform the verb from 'eat' to 'is eating', and insert the 'not' between its two parts. (For 'transformations' see Ch. I, 4.3.)

So far we have spoken of the vocabulary the child uses, his internal dictionary of words, gained by imitation, and the rules he devises for using it. These rules he devises as a linguist would, studying a hitherto unrecorded language. He looks at large numbers of examples and generalizes from them. An early rule the child acquires is that (as adults would say) subject precedes verb: *dog eat* and not *eat dog*, which means something different. This and other rules about word order are of first importance in English, because they determine the meaning. In Latin *amo puellam* and *puellam amo* both mean 'I love the girl'; but in English 'I love the girl' means one thing, 'the girl loves I' means quite another. Such rules of word order – subject before verb, determiner before noun, for instance – are, as we have seen (Ch. I, 3.3), rules of syntax.

There are also rules not affecting the order of words in a sentence, but making changes or 'inflections' in individual words as necessary. Thus for plurals we customarily add *s* – *slipper/s*; for past tenses we often add *ed* – *jump/ed*, etc. The child devises his rules for these changes in a similar way – by generalization from the examples he knows. Thus it is common to find the child saying *mans* not *men*, and *digged* for *dug*. He is unlikely to have heard either incorrect form, and thus must be applying rules he has deduced. Later on he will realize that there are certain irregular forms to which his rules do not apply. These are changes not in syntax but in accidence. Syntax is established before accidence. Thus in the example given above, *Daddy eat cake*, the word order is correct, but the child is not yet capable of producing the desired form *eats*.

There is a complication about the process of language acquisition as set out above, which we must now consider. We gave a very simple sentence, *Daddy eats cake*, as an example of what the child might imitate. But a child in the early stages couldn't imitate even that. He might imitate *Daddy cake*, or *cake*, or *daddy*. Parents do use a simplified language when talking directly to children. Even so, much of the language they use to them would be more complicated than this: *Daddy is eating his cake* would be much more likely, if only because a more natural way of making the statement. And again, children hear a good deal of language, between, say, their parents, that is not specially simplified for them, but from which they may learn.

Children deal with adult language by stripping it of inessentials, as we should do in writing a telegram. The child faced with *Daddy is eating his cake* may produce, if he is at that stage, *Daddy eat cake*. To take an actual example, quoted by Brown and Bellugi (1964), a mother's sentence *No you can't write on Mr. Cramer's shoe* was reduced by the child to *Write Cramer's shoe*. In both examples the child selects the grammatically important items, nouns, verbs, and adjectives, what are called 'content words', because they carry high 'information' content. He leaves out, on the other hand, structure words – words whose grammatical function is more important than the meaning they carry –, such as inflections, auxiliary verbs, articles, prepositions, and conjunctions.

We have just said that content words carry high 'information'. The word is used in the special sense derived from information theory: a word with high information content is one which it would be very difficult to guess from the context. Thus we could fairly easily guess *on* in *No you can't write on Mr. Cramer's shoe*, if it were left out, but it would be much harder to guess *shoe* or *write*. The fact that the child is beginning to attach a meaning in the external world to content words – he knows what a shoe is through everyday experience – is probably one reason why he chooses to repeat them rather than structure words like 'on'. There is no object or process 'on' in his world.

This is unlikely to be the only reason why he selects content words in preference to structure words, however, since it is a common experience that children have words of whose meaning they are ignorant. It seems likely to be more important that in adult speech the content words receive the main natural stresses:

'Daddy is éating the cáke.'
'Nó you cán't wríte on Mr. Crámer's shóe.'

They are the words or parts of words the child hears most clearly. At this stage his memory span is limited; he selects and repeats the words or syllables forced more on his attention. Presumably it is also his limited memory which leads him to repeat words from towards the end of the sentence he has just heard rather than words at the beginning (he did not, for instance, choose *can't write*). It is to be noted, however, that he repeats them in the right order, and not the last-heard first.

This ability to select significant linguistic features of adult language seems to be universal; that is, children learning whatever language have it. McNeill (1966) writes of a two-year-old Japanese girl, Izanami. In Japanese the subject of a sentence may be indicated by a 'post position', *ga*, as in 'The cat *ga* ate the goldfish'. Izanami was using *ga* frequently. This post position is used for specific statements; for general statements *wa* is used, as in 'Cats *wa* eat goldfish'. Izanami did not use *wa* frequently. Obviously she understood particular happenings, but had not yet generalized from them. i.e. she had not seen enough cats eating goldfish to know that it was characteristic of them.

This built-in capacity to select grammatically important words has been called a LAD or Language Acquisition Device (McNeill, 1966), or, the feminine form, a LAS, or Language Acquisition System (even linguists have their little jokes). As we have said, since it has only a limited memory span, it selects in telegraphic fashion the content words, partly because these have some meaning in the external world, partly because they are stressed in normal speech.

To summarize, LAD structures words. It recognizes the basic units or content words (noun, verb, adjective). It recognizes basic arrangements of words which tell us about relationships (subject with predicate, modifier with noun, and so on). It builds up a dictionary. It looks at the examples of usage it has access to, and from these devices rules for its own use. These rules are both basic and transformational: they are for making kernel structures and surface structures.

3. *LANGUAGE TEACHING AND LEARNING*

3.1 ADULTS TEACH LANGUAGE

Although children select and shorten adult utterances it seems that in any case adults deliberately adapt their language when speaking to children. We have no evidence of how well the child would learn if offered the language one adult uses to another, but it appears that many parents take care to utter well-formed sentences to children and to slow down their speed of utterance, and it is very common to substitute proper names and pronouns like *I* or *you* and to substitute proper names and kinship terms: *Mummy's coming*, for example, said by the mother herself.

There are quite specific instructional techniques adopted by parents. *Say bye bye* the child is told as Auntie disappears down the road. *That's Mr. Smith. Who is it?*—and the child has to repeat the name. But by far the most important teaching device employed is the expansion of the telegraphic utterances of the child: *Dog bark* might be expanded as *Yes the dog is barking*; *Johnny fall* as *Johnny fell down, didn't he?*, in each case as the mother interprets the sense intended. This would seem to be one of the main ways by which the child acquires transformations. In observations conducted by McNeill (1966) mothers were expanding the basic structures of their children's speech perhaps 30 per cent of the time.

3.2 CHILDREN PRACTISE LANGUAGE

A remarkable feature of the language learning of the young child is that he practises on his own. This phenomenon had not been studied until Weir (1962) recorded the pre-sleep monologues of her son Anthony while he was between two years four months and 2 years 6 months old. Everything he said between his being bade goodnight and his falling asleep was recorded, though he was of course unaware that this was being done and thought at first the microphone was a vacuum cleaner. Thus he was not attempting to communicate with anybody present: his speech consisted in part of imaginary dialogues with people he knew or toys of his, and in part of statements to no one in particular. During this time, without any apparent motive except delight in increasing his command of the language, he made many utterances, often characterized by such features as rhythmic patterning, assonance, alliteration. He corrected his own pronunciation, drilled himself in various sound distinctions, substituted various lexical items in a sentence pattern. In

> 'Like a piggy bank'
> 'Had a pink sheet on'
> 'The grey pig went out'

he is playing with sounds, as for instance 'pi-'. In the following he has a grammatical frame in which he is substituting nouns:

> 'What colour?'
> 'What colour blanket?'
> 'What colour mop?'
> 'What colour glass?'

He can also make more complicated substitutions or transformations:

> 'Like it'
> 'Don't like it'
> 'Like it daddy',

where there is a transformation to negative and back again. In

> 'Step on the blanket'
> 'Where is Anthony's blanket'

there is change from statement or command to question.

> Bobo go take off the hat
> Bobo took off that hat—

here a vocative imperative becomes a past indicative. The sentences have some resemblance to foreign-language learning drills; but they also resemble nursery rhymes and jingles. The poems which young children themselves produce have, as we shall see (Ch. 7, 3.6), very similar characteristics. In that all three help in language development they are performing a similar function.

Of course, language practice is going on continually in these years in the dialogues the child conducts with those around him, but this solitary practice is something new in our information about language acquisition.

4. UNDERSTANDING AND USE

4.1 DOES UNDERSTANDING PRECEDE USE?

Do children understand the language of others before they actually use language themselves? In one sense it is clear that they do. A little child who has not yet learned to speak will respond to such a request about a ball as *Give it daddy*). Indeed, it would be surprising if this were not the case, as animals, who never develop speech, show a similar understanding. Jan, the alsatian belonging to the present writer, will respond in the required ways to over twenty commands. In the case of the child and the dog we take their actions as evidence of their understanding because we have no other evidence.

Fond parents and fonder dog owners tell many stories of the 'understanding' of their charges. Whether it is an understanding of *language* is often not clear. So often the response may be to a whole situation or to a single non-linguistic element in the situation. If the father holds out his hand for the ball, it may be this action which prompts the child to give it him, and not the words he uses. The dog will respond in exactly the same fashion to 'Come and get it' and 'Don't come and get it', spoken when his mistress has placed his food dish on the floor. There are, of course, many cases in which it is clear that animal or child responds to verbal stimuli only. And in these cases it is common to speak of their 'understanding' language which they can't yet use.

This 'understanding', however, is very elementary – in some cases words might be replaced by whistles, as in sheep-dog trials, and the desired result still obtained. It is more appropriate to speak of 'understanding' when we are concerned with words in relation to one another, with the effect of their arrangement in simple grammatical patterns. There is no evidence that animals have any understanding of these: 'Give a paw', for instance, acts as a single stimulus. The dog could have been trained to shake hands at the word 'paw' alone. But young children certainly learn to understand them. The interesting question is whether they understand them before they can use them.

To test out the hypothesis that reception precedes production with regard to certain grammatical features, Fraser, Bellugi, and Brown (1963) took ten pairs of simple sentences, each pair demonstrating a different grammatical feature. These were such features as singular/plural marked by inflexions (e.g., the ending *s*), as in *the boy draws*/*the boys draw*: singular/plural marked by is/are; present progressive tense in contrast with past tense, and with future tense; and so on. It was hoped to test the ability to imitate, to comprehend, and to produce, such sentences, in twelve children of three (thirty-seven–forty-three months).

Imitation: The experimenter speaks the pair (e.g., *The sheep is jumping*/*The sheep are jumping*), and then asks the child to repeat each one after him. *Comprehension*: the child is shown two pictures – of one sheep jumping, and of two sheep jumping. The sentences are spoken twice, in turn, and he is asked to *point* to the appropriate picture in each case. *Production*: The sentences are spoken twice; the experimenter points to each in turn and requires the appropriate sentence to be *spoken* as he does so. It should be emphasized that three different pairs of sentences would be used to test the one feature, but that they would be of the same pattern.

From the results of the experiment it seems that the child-ren's Imitation was better than their Comprehension, and that their Comprehension was better than their Production. This supports the common assertion that understanding does in fact precede speaking, if we expect the children to know the meaning of what they say. But it seems that children often say things they don't understand, when they are just imitating from adults. The results of the experiment (that their Imita-tion was better than their Comprehension) also bears this out.

5. *TWO CONVERSATIONS*

Let us now turn to specific examples of children's speech in conversation with adults, in order to clarify and develop some of the general points in the above section. There now follow two transcripts of Edmund, one made at nineteen-and-a-half months and the other at twenty months. It may seem unneces-sary to quote two passages recorded so close together chrono-logically, but the boy's language is developing rapidly, and there are detectable advances in the second. One could not make this statement on the evidence of the passages alone — differences between them might be accidental, but in fact other recordings made at the same time confirm the development.

5.1   THE CONVERSATIONS

CONVERSATION I

Adult sitting on stool – row of holiday cards on ledge above –two photos of dogs – one the family pet, the other a Gains-borough print

EDMUND: (*playing with spade on carpet*)
                    lie down/lie down

ADULT: don't do that/not on the floor/Edmund/it's
                    for digging in the garden/no/come and show
                    it to Mo.
                    (*shows it*) isn't it lovely

EDMUND: lovely/lovely

ADULT: lovely

EDMUND: spade

ADULT: has the digger come back?

EDMUND: back/digger back/back/digger back

ADULT: has it

EDMUND: *(notices one of the cards)*

boat

ADULT: boats/this one/*(points to card)*

EDMUND: seaside/boat/car/car/car

ADULT: lots of cars

EDMUND: car/car by/*(gets muddled)* ball/buckeye(?)/

ball/ball/there's ballie/one

water/seaside/side

what's that/boat/boat/boat

ADULT: lots of boats

EDMUND: *(catches sight of photo of dog)*

doggie/doggie/see them doggie/see them/

doggie/doggie

ADULT: who is it

EDMUND: doggie/doggie

ADULT: it's not just a doggie though/it's *our* doggie

EDMUND: our doggie

ADULT: but what's her name

EDMUND: *(laughs)*

ADULT: what's the name of the doggie

EDMUND: name doggie

ADULT: it's Minna

EDMUND: it's Minna/what's that *(hook on the back of*

photo)

ADULT: to hang it up by

EDMUND: by

ADULT: to hang the picture up/no/don't spoil it

EDMUND: what's that

ADULT: put it back

EDMUND: back

ADULT: there

F.L.—5

EDMUND: here you are Min/Minna/see them Minna/ what's that . . . doggie/there's doggie/there's doggie/there's doggie (*has noticed other picture*)

ADULT: lovely little doggies/mummy dog/baby dog/ mummy dog/baby dog

EDMUND: one

ADULT: two/two doggies

EDMUND: doggie/two doggies

ADULT: put it back

EDMUND: back/what's that/tick tock/

ADULT: microphone

EDMUND: phone/microphone (*distorted by handling of it*)

ADULT: no leave it/you'll hurt it/don't touch read the book/read the book

EDMUND: book/(*mutters*) don't want it

ADULT: don't want it/has the digger come back yet/ has the digger come/digger

EDMUND: digger/digger/digger/come here doggie/ come here digger/come here digger/come here/come here digger/come here digger/come

ADULT: come here digger

EDMUND: come here/come here

ADULT: come here/gotcha/got you

EDMUND: tape/tape/tape/here's tape/push

ADULT: yes that's the tape

EDMUND: push . . . (*tape goes off*)

CONVERSATION 2

Before and during dinner

EDMUND: where's piggie

MOTHER: O piggie/all right

EDMUND: scarecrow/here's scarecrow/here's scarecrow/ here's scarecrow/here's scarecrow/here's scarecrow (*looking at picture drawn by mother*)

GRANDMA: Oh dear / are you going to draw a scarecrow

EDMUND: scarecrow

GRANDMA: Edmund draw a scarecrow

EDMUND: here's   scarecrow / here's   scarecrow / here's
scarecrow

GRANDMA: Edmund draw it

EDMUND: I draw it

GRANDMA: Oh dear

EDMUND: here's scarecrow (*all papers pushed off onto
floor*)

GRANDMA: they're all on the floor now / going to pick it
up

EDMUND: down now (*croons*)

GRANDMA: you're tired

MOTHER: he is isn't he

GRANDMA: do you want to go to bed

MOTHER: want to go to sleep / is daddy asleep

EDMUND: walkie / Moey's walkie (*Moey: Grandmother*)

GRANDMA: Moey's going a walkie / Moey's knitting

EDMUND: knitting

GRANDMA: knitting with knitting pins

EDMUND: pins / it's mine

MOTHER: daddy's gone to play football Edmund

EDMUND: walkie / sleep / sleep / money daddy / daddy
sleep / daddy sleep / daddy sleep

MOTHER: no daddy's playing football

EDMUND: football

MOTHER: football

EDMUND: ball

GRANDMA: kick it / catch it

MOTHER: kick it / kick it

EDMUND: pudding / it's mine

MOTHER: do you want some dinner Edmund

EDMUND: it's mine pinny (*really pin*)

GRANDMA: it's your penny

EDMUND: it's yours

MOTHER: pin, not penny

EDMUND: penny pin

GRANDMA: you're an echo

EDMUND: echo/dinner

MOTHER: mummy's cooking you some peas and potatoes

EDMUND: tatoes peas

MOTHER: and some gravy/and some meat

EDMUND: a swingie/round and round/tapes round that/
tapes round that

GRANDMA: it's a tape recorder

EDMUND: 'torder/peas have it

GRANDMA: don't cry/what did you say Edmund

EDMUND: peas

GRANDMA: (*misunderstands*) please what

EDMUND: want peas
(*eats dinner*)

MOTHER: have you finished Edmund/oh you want to
eat these bits do you/whoops/scrape it/is that
nice

EDMUND: it's rabbit/carrots/(*sees pictures on the dish*)

MOTHER: yes that's right/he's eating a carrot/isn't he
nice/there's a fly with a hat on

EDMUND: fly/fly

MOTHER: butterfly/that's it/butterfly

EDMUND: rabbit/it's rabbit

MOTHER: they're having a picnic/there's one there
going swimswim

EDMUND: balloon/boonie/swim swim/dinner time/
dinner/dins/din

MOTHER: you've eaten it all now and you didn't want
the rest

EDMUND: want peas more/want peas/um

MOTHER: you don't really want it/it's cold

EDMUND: want a biscuit/want a drink

MOTHER: want dinner

EDMUND: I'll get your dinner back then

EDMUND: *(laughs)* here's fly/here's fly/dinner/tatoe tatoe tatoe

MOTHER: meat/don't you want it now

EDMUND: pudding/*(general laughter)* tatoes/want down now there's biscuit/want down now/ want down now

MOTHER: what do you say/dow....

EDMUND: down please/want a drink football

5.2 ANALYSIS

The recordings make for convenient comparison, in that Edmund's contribution in each case is about 120 words.

5.2.1 SENTENCES

We use the term 'sentence' here for any word or group of words which seems a 'free utterance' (able to stand by itself), and which is separated by silence, however brief, from other groups of words. In the first conversation there are eighty-three sentences, twenty-four of two words, six of three words, and one of four words. In the second conversation there are seventy utterances, twenty-five of two words, six of three words. (For these purposes *where's*, *it's*, etc. are counted as one word.) In other words, in the first, the earlier, conversation, there is a greater number of single words used as sentences. This one would expect.

5.2.2 CONTENT WORDS

In Ch. I, 4.1 above we used the term 'content words' for nouns, verbs, and adjectives, which carry the 'content' of the utterance. Nearly always their function is that of naming. Edmund sees the picture post-cards, and describes what he sees: *car*, *dog* (*doggie*), *boat*, *ball* (*ballie*); these words, together with *digger* (his spade) form the bulk of his nouns in this conversation and are repeated frequently. In the second conversation the naming function of nouns continues (*pin*, *'corder*, *scarecrow*), but they refer also to abstract things which are objects of desire or states of mind (*walkie*/*sleep*/*sleep*); when he mentions *peas*, Edmund is not learning, or reinforcing his knowledge of the name; he knows it, and it has become synonymous with the objects he wants.

Let us turn to verbs. In the first place they are mainly constituents of formulas, phrases that he must have learnt whole by imitation. Thus his favourite is *what's that* (five times). We can see this process happening when he repeats – *it's Minna*, direct from the adult. *Come here* is similarly a formula, but he has learnt to change the next word at will (*doggie*/ *digger*). Likewise *here you are Min* is doubtless a formula with the dog's name added. The use of *here's* and *there's* (*there's ballie, here's tape*) are extensions of the naming function of the single word. He has the phrase *see them* (*Minna*/ *doggie*) meaning *Look at Minna*/*dog*. The most advanced verb phrase he uses is *don't want it*, a negative using two verbs, probably learnt as a formula.

In the second conversation we again find the formulas with variations: *here's scarecrow*, but he can now employ *where* also: *where's piggie*. His most advanced sentence is *I draw it*, in part modelled on the adult's *Edmund draw it*. He ventures out from formulas and thus produces non-standard forms like *peas have it* and *want peas more*.

In the second conversation the *I* substituted for Edmund is notable; he transforms the adult *It's your penny* into *it's yours*; he can handle *it's mine*, but not *it's mine penny*. Adjectives only occur by direct imitation: *lovely, two*.

5·2·3   STRUCTURE WORDS

In neither passage are structure words significant. There are no auxiliary verbs except in the formula *don't want it*; *by* occurs by direct imitation (with a further *by* in a maze).

5·3   THE ADULT-CHILD INTERACTION

The adult has many functions in relation to the child – to keep the child happy, adequately fed and entertained, to prevent the carpet getting damaged. In both the conversations the child is also being instructed in language. Thus in both conversations the child's utterances are being expanded:

EDMUND: car / car / car
ADULT: lots of cars

EDMUND: Moeys walkie
ADULT: Moeys going a walkie

EDMUND: fly / fly
ADULT: butterfly / that's it butterfly

Elsewhere greater particularity is being required:

EDMUND: doggie
ADULT: it's not just a doggie though / it's *our* doggie

EDMUND: our doggie

EDMUND: there's doggie
ADULT: mummy dog / baby dog / mummy dog / baby dog

The adult's expansion of the child's statement also serves as a reinforcement to him, in that it convinces him he has been understood.

EDMUND: don't want it
ADULT: don't want it

Quite specific correction may take place:

EDMUND: it's my penny
ADULT: pin, not penny
EDMUND: penny pin

In contrast to the adult expansions of the child's language there are the child's contractions of the adult language:

isn't it lovely	lovely / lovely / lovely
has the digger come back	digger back / back / digger back
it's our doggie	our doggie
what's the name of the	name doggie
doggie	
Moeys knitting	knitting
knitting with knitting pins	pins
tape recorder	torder

It is to be noted that Edmund is contracting the language he hears according to the principles of stress and recency which we spoke of above (Section 2). It is always stressed words that are repeated, and words towards the end of the sentence. Edmund repeats mostly nouns; but he repeats the adjective 'lovely', which is stressed when occurring terminally – and the possessive pronoun *our*, because the adult puts deliberate stress on it.

5.4 SYNTAX AND ACCIDENCE

We can think of grammar as consisting of two parts. The first is syntax – the way we arrange our words in relation to one another: *said John/John said*. The second is accidence – the alterations we make to words themselves: *book/books, break/broke, I/me*. Now Edmund's syntax is, within its limits, usually correct, as in:

> 'here's scarecrow'
> 'it's mine penny'
> 'what's that'
> 'I draw it',

but not : in

> 'want peas more'.

His accidence is, of course, very limited; in verbs to a simple present – *want/draw*, etc.; and he has yet to learn to inflect nouns – singulars for plurals, for instance. This does not show up as yet, since he doesn't use language that requires this agreement. The limitations on the use of 'mine' are not understood; and so on. As we shall see in more detail later, the development of syntax will continue to be ahead of that of accidence.

6. *THE DEVELOPMENT OF LANGUAGE*

6.1 A GLANCE AHEAD

We have looked at an early stage in the acquisition of language. From this normal children develop rapidly, till by the time they are three-and-a-half or four their language is quite well pronounced. It is often said by linguists and psychologists that by that age they possess the main grammatical structures of English. It is not usually clear what is meant by this in detail, but some indication is given of the type of structures, possessed by at least some children, in the examples of Chapter V. Their pronunciation of the language is also fairly standard, if that is the pronunciation of those who surround them: 'by the fourth year, the child's phonological system closely approximates the model, and the remaining deviations are usually corrected by the time the child enters school' (Ervin and Miller, 1963, p. 116).

6.2 For Whom: for What Purpose?

Let us now leave for the moment the matter of the formal qualities of children's language, and ask two related questions: For whom is it intended? and What purpose is it serving?

To answer the first question we need to extend the model on page 21. Its final term was 'Language' – influenced by Subject, Addressee, and Context. But of course the Addressee functions in the model not only as an influence on the language, but as its recipient. Thus we need to add:

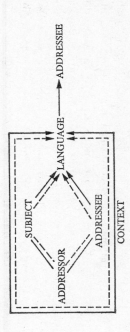

But, it may be agreed, all language does not assume an addressee. There is the language of private diaries; of exclamations and oaths; of mutterings under one's breath; of speaking one's thoughts aloud, unconscious of anyone's overhearing; even of some poetry which is meditative, self-analytical, and so private in its symbolism that it seems the writer is indifferent to an audience. Yet even here, apart from involuntary exclamations and obsessive mutterings, there is an Addressee – the Self. And indeed much language which appears to have only Self as Addressee is really intended for others, whether the Addressor is aware of it or not.

LANGUAGE ──→ ADDRESSEE $\begin{cases} \text{SELF} \\ \text{OTHERS} \end{cases}$

There is the famous remark by Gwendoline in *The Importance of Being Earnest* about her diary: it is a young girl's record of her private thoughts and feelings, and therefore intended for publication. However obscure their work, poets tend to expect an audience, even if it is of the very select few. Blake's work, as a whole, is couched in a whole mythology of private symbols, but its meaning seemed clear as day to him, and he was bewildered by the lack of comprehension it met with. Even so, we can make a rough distinction between language for self and language for others.

This is associated with two needs language serves – the need to express, and the need to communicate. A writer who produces a poem may do so because he is under pressure from an experience he has undergone; he feels he must verbalize it, and attempt to understand it for himself, whether anybody else does so or not. This is obviously different from a teacher's explaining the same poem to a class, where, unless he communicates the meaning, amongst other things, he has failed. The first is using language for self, the second language for others.

6.3 SPEECH FOR SELF AND OTHERS

Piaget makes a distinction of this kind in describing the speech of young children, a distinction between 'egocentric' and 'socialized' speech. Vygotsky (1965) sums up the differences between the two:

In egocentric speech, the child talks only about himself, takes no interest in his interlocutor, does not try to communicate, expects no answer and often does not care whether anyone listens to him. It is similar to a monologue in play: The child is thinking aloud, keeping up a running accompaniment, as it were, to whatever he may be doing. In socialised speech, he does attempt an exchange with others – he begs, commands, threatens, conveys information, asks questions (p. 15).

We may easily illustrate both types of speech. In the following transcription a boy of two years nine months is playing, taking animals to school in a 'wheel van'. It is in good measure speech-for-self, in that he is absorbed in his commentary, explaining to himself what is happening, as it were. But he constantly uses speech-for-others to his sister Zoe, mainly instructing her to keep her hands off, and to his father, encouraging him to play. He also answers his mother's question at the beginning:

MOTHER: do they do anything else at school

GUY: yes/sums/sums/going school Zoe/going school/ going school/that one going wheel van/in wheel van/no/Brm (imitating van)/legs in it/going school/going school/that little little big lamb/ going school/that big lamb/go school Zoe/go school/no touch it/doing writing/go away/go away/no touch it/here school/here school/yes/ brm here/that/that school/no touch it/go away/go away/play daddy/what's that for/ what's that for/

The terms 'egocentric' and 'socialized' are not very happy as translated into English. 'Egocentric' might seem to imply the child is a selfish little beast, whereas no such moral judgement is intended. Vygotsky also criticized the term 'socialized', as though the speech 'had been something else before becoming social' (p. 19), and suggested 'communicative'. We have suggested above that the distinction between adult language for self and for others is not an absolute one. Vygotsky made a similar point concerning Piaget's analysis. He carried out some experiments in which children using speech in play were deprived of the feeling that they were being understood, by giving them an 'audience' of deaf or foreign children. They either ceased talking at all or talked very much less. Vygotsky concluded that 'The primary function of speech in both children and adults is communication, social contact. The earliest speech of the child is therefore essentially social' (p. 19). This language, whatever we call it, is the only one the child has; he makes no distinction between self and others as Addressee. It develops in two ways. One way it becomes the language he uses to communicate with others; the other way it becomes silent, goes within, becomes inner speech or thought. We can see how this may happen from Guy's monologue above.

We have spoken so far about the language of the child in terms of who is the Addressor, and we find that the Addressor is both self and others; but if others do not listen, then he ceases to talk to self. The child to whom no one listens grows silent. And if he grows silent he ceases to think externally; and this will affect his later internal speech. We should, however, bear in mind that Vygotsky's experiments do not show that the child *never* addresses self alone; the pre-sleep monologues of Weir (1962), described earlier in the chapter, in fact demonstrate that the does do so – though we should bear in mind that these monologues can be regarded as practice for a future audience. This exception focuses our attention on one limitation in both Piaget and Vygotsky: they talk about the language of young children without very much reference to particular situations; and as we have pointed out in Chapter II, the situations influence the language produced. And the dialogues quoted in later chapters of this book (for instance, Ch. VII) show considerable social reaction between adult and children of three-and-a-half or four. Piaget finds children to have a large proportion of egocentric talk because he views them in situations, group play, for instance, where egocentric talk is likely.

It is undeniable that young children are very self-involved; and in one sense almost all their talk is 'egocentric', speech for self, in that through it the child is attempting to fulfil *his* desires, discover *his* identity, build up *his* picture of the world. But he does not do this only by talking to self, but by inter-action with others, including adults. To find out what he thinks he must find out what others think, and what others think about what he thinks.

7. *SUMMARY*

Certain of the child's first sounds resembling words are selected, shaped, and reinforced by the adults surrounding him. At about a year old he may utter single words. He imitates words and formulas, but then begins to utter sentences he can never have heard; he is developing grammatical rules for use, by means of his Language Acquisition Device. He simplifies adult sentences by sorting out the content words; and adults in turn expand his sentences. He understands, before he can use, particular words and phrases. His syntax is in advance of his accidence. The monologues he comes to utter in play are the means whereby he uses words to think externally, and later develops into inner speech or thought.

CHAPTER IV

LANGUAGE AND REALITY

Language has a variety of functions. In Chapter I we glanced at some of them, and we shall be going into further detail in Chapter VII. For the moment we shall be looking at two of them: language as a means of thinking, and language as a means of building up a picture of reality. Needless to say, these two are closely connected.

1. *LANGUAGE AND THOUGHT*

It is commonly agreed that there is a close relationship between language and thought.

1.1 THOUGHT WITHOUT WORDS

Is thought possible without words? This will depend to some extent on our definition of 'thought'. One definition given by the *O.E.D.* is 'the formation and arrangement of ideas' in the mind. As for the formation of ideas, we may form the idea of a picture – a dining room, an Eskimo, a camel – instantly; and we may, indeed, arrange these ideas together by imagining a camel walking across a dining room in company with an Eskimo. In our minds are images or symbols of the real things. At this level there is no need of words; we are thinking in pictures. Much thought like this goes on in dreams, and perhaps occurs in animals also. We do not know whether a dog growling in his sleep does so because in his mind a larger dog is stealing his largest bone, but it is possible.

The characteristic of thought we are focusing on here is its symbolic quality: Piaget calls it 'internalized imitation' (1968,

p. 90) – the mind is imitating objects and happenings outside it. Piaget, in explaining his view that thought originates independently of language, illustrates another way in which young children use non-verbal symbols – symbolic play, in which a child represents something without words. One of Piaget's children represented himself sleeping: 'He grabbed the corner of the sheet firmly in his hand, put his thumb in his mouth, closed his eyes, and while still sitting, smiled broadly' (p. 90). In this case the child represents his own behaviour symbolically; he may also imitate that of others – a daughter of Piaget imitated, without anger, the tantrums of a small friend after he had left. Clearly, another way of representing these events would be by the symbols we call words, and this is exactly what we have done by the fact of describing them. Piaget comments: 'We can say, therefore, that a symbolic function exists which is broader than language and encompasses both the system of verbal signs and that of symbols in the strict sense. It can thus be argued that the source of thought is to be found in the symbolic function' (p. 91).

Piaget's argument, then, is that the capacity to symbolize things to oneself and others is what we mean by thought; and that this precedes language, language being only one means of symbolizing. 'As language is only a particular form of the symbolic function and as the individual symbol is certainly simpler than the collective sign (*i.e. language-signs about which we agree collectively*), it is permissible to conclude that thought precedes language, and that language confines itself to profoundly transforming thought by helping it to attain its forms of equilibrium by means of more advanced schematization and a more mobile abstraction' (p. 92).

Thus thought is possible without language, but only on a very primitive level; language profoundly transforms it. Deaf children, who, be it noted, have language, and are thus able to use some of its resources for thinking, are nevertheless handicapped. Lewis (1968, p. 66), surveying the research, accepts that deaf children may 'think without language', or 'to be more exact with little or no use of language', but concludes that over a wide range of cognitive tasks the achievement of deaf children is impaired by the inadequacy of their language.

1.2 CONCEPT FORMATION

Let us return to our camel in the dining-room with his Eskimo. Without words we should have great difficulty in communicating with the reader about them. We could draw them, or film them, or we could have people dress up as a camel and an Eskimo, construct a stage set of a dining room, and present the scene to readers drawn from all parts, but it is doubtful whether this would be worth the trouble. Further, the Eskimo would be a Non-linguistic Man (see Ch. VII, 3), so he could only demonstrate to us a limited number of emotions towards the camel. He could embrace it or slap it, and we should know what he meant. But if we wanted to say 'Camels are normally the most surly of beasts, but this one is only moderately surly', we should be in difficulties, because moderate surliness is difficult for someone acting the part of a camel to mime.

Language, on the other hand, says the same thing, less picturesquely, perhaps, but much more exactly, much more economically. And one of the reasons it does this is its quality of abstraction and generalization. Even if we succeeded in getting the whole elaborate pantomime just described into production it could only give a message about one camel. If we wanted to make the message apply to all camels we should have to have representations of them there. Similarly, if we wanted to communicate the meaning of 'beasts', defined by the O.E.D. (in the singular) as 'a living being; an animal', we should have to have representations of all living beings, all animals there. If we left a single class out — aardvarks, for instance — 'beasts' would mean all living beings except aardvarks.

The illustration may seem comic, but its intention is serious, because the development of such generalizations as 'camels' and 'beasts' is essential for thinking beyond a primitive level, and one which can only be carried out effectively through language. It is known as 'concept formation'. An excellent simple account, to which the reader is referred, is given by Stones (1966, p. 144). He defines a concept as follows.

A concept is an abstraction from objects, situations, or events of the attributes these phenomena have in common. The words we use symbolize or stand for those concepts. The idea of *tree* is a concept. *Tree* refers not to one thing but to a class of things. From the multitude of different types of tree; the oak, the ash, the eucalyptus, the palm, the fir, the pine, we abstract the essential similarities and ignore the inessential differences. We call them all *tree*. Tree is a generic term. That is, it does not refer to one thing in particular, it refers to all such things in general.

Children are making elementary attempts in this direction when they call each man they see *daddy*, or each animal *doggie*. This is known as 'stimulus generalization'. But they will learn that *daddy* and *doggie* are only particular instances of the concept *man* or *animal*. Of course, words like *daddy* and *doggie* are themselves concepts, in that they describe a class of person and animal; there are countless individual fathers and individual dogs.

The possession of concepts is so much a part of our thinking that it is very difficult to imagine what it would be like to be without them. They provide us with, in Piaget's words, an 'advanced schematization' – a classificatory system by which we are able to relate experiences one to another. It may be that the reader of this book had not met 'aardvark' before. It is a type of animal. For most purposes we do not need to know more; we are able to deal with the concept fairly abstractly. But if we did not hold this concept of 'animal', the only thing we could do about the aardvark would be to imagine it in our minds, having seen it. We might perceive in it similarities to the armadillo, since an aardvark is 'an insectivorous quadruped, one of the Edentata, intermediate between Armadillos and Ant-eaters'. This would be by 'stimulus-generalization' – in much the same way as some dogs bite all men in uniform.

But we should be quite incapable of recognizing it as an animal, much less as an insectivorous quadruped. Concepts store our experiences, and, further, cut away details to enable us to see essentials. Most of the time all that matters to us about the aardvark is that it is an animal. To another aardvark, of course, much more detailed (but non-conceptualized) knowledge is necessary.

Concept acquisition through language is essential for thinking beyond an elementary level. Of course, concepts are man-made, in the sense that they do not exist in nature. Take the concepts associated with time. Why should there be sixty seconds in a minute, sixty minutes in an hour, and twenty-four hours in one day? Only because man has chosen to divide time up in that way. It is true that in earlier clocks, such as the grandfather, the pendulum takes one second to complete its swing; but that is only because it is deliberately made 39·1393 inches long to cause it to do this, If there were thirty seconds in one minute (as we understand it), the pendulum would have to be over thirteen feet (156·5572 inches) long, which would be very inconvenient. But if there were 120 seconds in the same minute the pendulum would only need to be 9·7848 inches long, which would be much more convenient, if we wished the pendulum beat to coincide with our measure of time. Even obvious concepts like 'man' and 'woman' are human creations, in the sense that we choose to think their sex is the most notable feature. If we lived in a society of giraffe-like people, where height was the main thing that mattered (if you couldn't reach your food from tall trees you would be in difficulties), we might instead have 'talls' and 'shorts' as the basic classification. In the Norfolk (England) expression that someone or something is 'neither he, she, nor old woman' we have a humorous challenge to the bi-sexual division of mankind. It is in this sense that man creates the world in which he lives by means of language; and he teaches his children the concepts he has found useful. Piaget uses the term 'the construction of reality' to describe the way the child builds up in himself an awareness of these concepts –

of, first of all, the 'schemes of the permanent object, space, time, and causality'.

None of these categories is given at the onset, and the child's initial universe is entirely centred in his own body, and action in an egocentricism as total as it is unconscious (for lack of consciousness of the self). In the course of the first eighteen months, however, there occurs a kind of Copernican revolution, or, more simply, a kind of general decentring process whereby the child eventually comes to regard himself as an object among others in a universe that is made up of permanent objects (that is, structured in a spatio-temporal manner)) and in which there is at work a causality that is both localized in space and objectified in things (Piaget and Inhelder, 1969, p. 13).

It is the construction of reality by language that we wish to look at in more detail but rather in linguistic and literary than in psychological terms.

2. *THE CONSTRUCTION OF REALITY*

2.1 'REALITY' AND MAN

We have spoken of the way in which children build up concepts from objects, situations, events, and other concepts. Piaget refers to this process as the child's construction of reality. What this means is that children internalize, make part of their own thinking, the ways of thought, the view of the world, of their elders. We have seen, however, that this 'reality' itself is man made; and the question then arises as to how far it can be said to coincide with any reality outside man. This, in the last resort unanswerable, question we shall consider later. For the moment let us look at the child's construction of reality, using the terms in the sense just defined.

2.2 FROM INNOCENCE TO EXPERIENCE

When I was a child I spake as a child,
I understood as a child, I thought as a child. . . .

Piaget, quoted in the section above, uses an image to describe the general process of acquiring a mature view of reality –

that of a Copernican Revolution. Copernicus was the seven-
teenth-century astronomer who formulated the (current)
view that planets, including Earth, move round the sun and
not that the whole universe revolves round Earth. In a similar
way the child comes to realize that everything does not revolve
round, does not exist merely for, him. His thinking becomes
less egocentric. In the process the child makes interpretations
according to the information he has, fitted into the inner
schematization he has so far developed at a particular stage.
For instance, a child of six asks why a marble is rolling down-
hill, and is told that it is on an incline. He is not satisfied and
asks 'It knows you are down there?' (Piaget, 1968, p. 24). This
is *animism*, whereby inanimate objects are endowed with
human characteristics, just as nursery toys are. The boy has
developed to the stage where he understands something of
human motive but not of physical principles.

2.2.1   *'Songs of Innocence and of Experience'*

Poets and writers have been fascinated by this period of early
childhood, which Blake calls the state of innocence. In his
Songs of Innocence Blake constantly returns to the joy he sees
everywhere about it. In 'Infant Joy' joy is personified as a baby
'but two days old'. In the 'Nurse's Song' 'The little ones leaped
and shouted and laughed/and all the hills echoed.' Children
are like this in ideal conditions, when surrounded by security
and love; in *Songs of Innocence* there is scarcely a poem in
which a benign guardian figure does not keep watch over the
children — the mother, the nurse, the shepherd, the 'old folk'.
Blake is of course aware that children without these conditions are miserable, i.e. when the guardian figures are hostile
or non-existent:

Is this a holy thing to see
In a rich and fruitful land —
Babes reduced to misery,
Fed with cold and usurous hand?

('Holy Thursday', *Songs of Experience*.)

Wordsworth similarly sees the joy of early childhood, speaking of it in the 'Immortality Ode' as a time

> when meadow, grove and stream,
> The earth, and every common sight,
>   To me did seem
> Apparelled in celestial light.

But for such writers the attraction of this early world is not only that it represents for them a kind of Eden. It is in the freshness with which the child views our own familiar world – in the very fact that he has not yet acquired the inner schematization we were discussing in the previous section. He stands outside received opinion. And thus many of his remarks delight by surprising us. There is a doubtless true story of a child of four who asked what God had for dinner. Her mother replied that God didn't have any dinner. 'Won't he be hungry?' the girl asked. Her mother, a little perplexed, tried to explain: 'Well, you see, God doesn't have any body.' 'You mean his legs join onto his head?' asked the girl. This story throws up the ambiguity of the mother's language, and is incidentally an interesting comment on how children may see adults – drawings by young children frequently show legs descending straight from the head. All parents can tell similar stories of their own children.

Wordsworth was so impressed by such insights of the young child that he proclaimed him

> Mighty Prophet! Seer blest!
> On whom those truths do rest
> Which we are toiling all our lives to find
>
>   ('Immortality Ode')

though some people might think that is going a bit far. Blake drew on the freedom of the child from accepted opinions, resulting in unconscious insights, to put into his mouth apparently naïve remarks which cut at the very fabric of society – in 'Holy Thursday' (*Experience*), for instance, or 'The Little Vagabond':

Dear Mother, dear Mother, the Church is cold,
But the Ale-house is healthy, and pleasant and warm;
Besides I can tell where I am used well,
Such usage in Heaven will never do well.

The argument of the poem – why can't God and the Devil be friends? why can't all the pleasure and humanity of the ale-house be part of religion? – is a savage satiric comment on the joylessness of much puritan religion as Blake knew it:

Then the parson might preach, and drink, and sing,
And we'd be as happy as birds in the spring.

What Piaget calls the construction of reality Blake would call a progress from Innocence to Experience. Of course by his Experience Blake means much more than Piaget's 'reality': for him it is the whole adult universe, not only with its concepts and ways of thought, but with its guilt, misery, and tyranny in contrast with the innocence, joy, and security of early childhood. For Blake this whole universe is man made – its concepts, its institutions, its gods:

The ancient Poets animated all sensible objects with Gods or Geniuses, calling them by the names and adorning them with the properties of woods, rivers, mountains, lakes, cities, nations and whatever their enlarged and numerous senses could perceive. . . . And at length they pronounc'd that the Gods had ordered such things

Thus men forgot that All deities reside in the human breast. (*The Marriage of Heaven and Hell*, Nonesuch edn., p. 195.)

Blake's view of the nature of reality may be summed up in the title of one of his poems, 'The Human Abstract' – it is constructed of man's abstracts – or concepts.

The Gods of earth and sea
Sought thro' Nature to find this Tree;
But their search was all in vain:
There grows one in the human brain.

The human brain is the source of the world of Experience. Blake is saying that we live in the world our minds create. This world is not, however, necessarily evil. The tiger, breaking out of the 'forests of the night', is a symbol of the richer, fuller, more imaginative life man can create (see Wilkinson, 1958, pp. 51–2).

2.2.2 'The Foundling'

By way of further illustration let us turn now from the great poetry of Blake to a minor modern work, *The Foundling*, a radio play by Peter Gurney (1965). Here we see a young child constructing reality for himself very much in Piagetian terms. The Prologue states the general theme of the play, the child's losing his apparent power to manipulate and order the world:

> The loss was losing what he had,
> And what he had can never be replaced
> At any cost.
> For he has lost his power the world
> To make, the sun to bind and loose,
> The hills to move.

The story is about a young child, Stephen, who sometimes plays in a country church near his home. On his way there he crosses a stream:

> If I can jump over
> Without getting wet
> Then the sun won't go out.

And this sets him musing:

> How did they find out the name of the sun
> When they couldn't get there?

To his 'enlarged and numerous senses', to use Blake's terms, everything is alive. On his way through the churchyard

> He thinks the dead are lying in their houses
> – Like a sentry to attention in his box,

– Like the weather figures; or cuckoos in their clocks.

He approaches the church with apprehension:

Here the gargoyles wait, with dripping fangs,

but he feels safer inside, and imagines that the carvings speak to him. One of his games is to 'play at parsons' from the pulpit:

> Dearly beloved
> We have run away like lost sheep
> Have mercy on us, miserable fenders.

An old tramp who has been sleeping in the church disturbs him. There is no doubt in his mind who this is:

> I knew at once in terror
> The old man with the beard,
> White hair, white eyes, the stick,
> The trailing garment.

The tramp, innocent of his mistake, swears him to secrecy for his own reasons:

> I went home, delirious with honour,
> Far too dazed to play. The secret
> Forced my face to smile, time and again,
> And once in the middle of tea,
> Compelled my voice to laugh out loud,
> But I would tell them nothing.

The following Sunday, at morning service, the child suddenly realizes that all the creatures in the church, carvings, paintings, and figures in stained glass, know the secret:

> As I sat between my giant parents
> Beneath the rector in his tower
> I suddenly knew that *they* knew too –
> The corbel king with secret smiling knew:
> The bosses on the beams, of spikey sun,
> Three-headed man, and Galilean crew,

Fox preaching to geese, and man with toothache,
Dolphin, donkey, dog and centaur, *knew.*

At the closing hymn, the Hymn of St. Francis, they all burst
into a great symphony of praise, heard only by the boy:

And as the hymn proceeded
Came the voice
Of centaur, dolphin,
Ring dove sweet, and donkey coarse,
Singing.
The stall arms puffed their pigeon fists
The stained glass rang with light.
And then the angels, prone in the swirling air
Upon their harps and symphonies struck out
Upon their shawms and serpents blew.
And in the roof and on the walls
And from the misereres sad
They sang and played
The boy with bloated cheeks and bloated tongue,
Noah, whilst making his ten thousandth ark,
The carpenter, while making his unfinished self,
The king and wormy queen upraised,
The bear, the pig with bagpipes: praised.

But there are other creatures in the church who do not join in,
the evil ones who are imprisoned in the woodwork and stone.
These have previously threatened the boy:

I am Belial, wrapped in pain,
And struggling dreadful against the grain,
But if I could get free –
I am the Devil, immured alive,
Bound in cordage, five times five,
But if I could get loose –
If God were dead,
I'd break your head
And spread your blood like jam on bread.

The unthinkable happens. The boy finds the tramp dead in the crypt, and to him this means that the will of God, which has kept the evil ones in their prisons, is broken. He flees in terror from the church. The narrator comments:

> The fear of a child
> Is perfect. He can never say
> That the sun will rise on another day;
> Nor that his mother, who goes outside,
> Has not, by that effacement, died.

The child runs away and is lost. Eventually he is found and it is explained to him that it was not God but an old tramp who had died. Thus he goes to church expecting a great symphony of rejoicing at this news:

> And I heard *nothing*.
> In the church, noisy with ragged voices,
> I stood in a great silence. . . .
> And as the congregation sang
> In individual tones;
> All the created things were dumb,
> Like stocks and stones.

The play illustrates the way a young child makes sense of experience in terms of the information he possesses, and the schematization he has to process it with. He does not know the 'tramp', but he knows 'God', partly from pictures; he does not understand causality; he interprets 'miserable offenders' as 'miserable fenders' because they have a fender on the hearth at home: his thinking is animistic.

Writers and psychologists tend to lay a somewhat different emphasis on this period of early childhood. Writers look at its potentialities for joy, the unique privilege it has of looking at the world anew, like Adam and Eve in Eden. They thus often speak about its passing in terms of regret. Psychologists are necessarily thinking of the inadequacies of the schematization which exists at this time. Both viewpoints are valuable; they attempt to discern for us different aspects of the truth.

3. LANGUAGE, THOUGHT, AND REALITY

We have seen how young children may create a world of their own, governed by laws of magic rather than nature. We have also seen how they may move from the world into the world of what we call 'reality'. They 'construct reality', in Piaget's terms, and this reality is one divided up according to our adult concepts – of time, space, motion, causality. In one sense we are in the same position as the child: his limited schematization gives him a limited view of reality; ours is less limited, and gives us a wider notion of the real. But there are limitations to both views. And it seems that the language we use to express our concept has a considerable effect on our view of reality, and on our consequent behaviour.

The linguist who has had most influence on our thinking about 'the relation of habitual thought and behaviour to language' is Benjamin Lee Whorf (1966), who, in a series of papers, one with that title, collected together after his death, formulated the theories known as the 'Whorfian hypotheses'. He in turn acknowledged his debt to Sapir, whom he quotes:

Human beings do not live in the objective world alone, nor alone in the world of social activity as ordinarily understood, but are very much at the mercy of the particular language which has become the medium of expression for their society. It is quite an illusion to imagine that one adjusts to reality essentially without the use of language and that language is merely an incidental means of solving specific problems of communication or reflection. The fact of the matter is that the 'real world' is to a large extent unconsciously built up on the language habits of the group . . . We see and hear and otherwise experience very largely as we do because the language habits of our community predispose certain choices of interpretation.

Blake said, 'A fool sees not the same tree that a wise man sees.' Whorf would have phrased the thought differently: an Eskimo sees not the same snow as an Englishman sees. Whorf pointed out that the class 'snow' in English would seem far too general to an Eskimo to be of any use: the Eskimo has different words for falling snow, snow on the ground, packed snow, slushy snow, wind-driven flying snow, whatever the situation may be. In contrast, the Aztecs have apparently only one word for cold, ice, and snow. The language of the Hopi (American) Indians 'has one noun that covers everything or being that flies, with the exception of birds, which class is denoted by another noun. . . . The Hopi actually call insect, airplane, and aviator, all by the same word, and feel no difficulty about it. This class would seem too general to us' (p. 216).

The problem is not that certain things can be said in one language, and not in another. Rather it is how easily and habitually are they said, for these will determine the tendency of thought. The English speaker does not habitually recognize the distinctions in types of snow. Experiment by Brown and Lennenberg (1954), for instance, has shown that colours for which we have single names are recognized more easily than others. It has been pointed out that the lack of words for such concepts as 'snow' is comparatively trivial; but that the word 'conscience' in French should stand for 'consciousness' and 'conscience' in English indicates a more fundamental difference in thinking. The present writer had this brought home to him forcibly at an international conference, when an argument between a French and an English delegate turned on a misunderstanding about this word.

Whorf studied North American Indian languages such as Hopi, and found the grammatical organization to be different from that of most 'standard average European' (S.A.E.) languages; and this different organization implied a different view of reality. In S.A.E. there are nouns and verbs, things and actions. The nouns 'exist', long term; and the verbs are what happens to them, short term. Whorf asks if 'strike, turn, run' are verbs, because they refer to short-lasting events or actions, why is 'first' a noun? Why are 'lightning, spark, wave, eddy, pulsation, flame, storm, phase, cycle, spasm, noise, emotion' nouns? In contrast, why are 'keep, adhere, extend, project, continue, persist, grow, dwell' verbs? They are long-lasting phenomena like 'house' and 'man'. Whorf is pointing out that there are means of classification different from the ones we employ, and he demonstrates from the Hopi language where 'lightning, wave, flame, meteor, puff of smoke, pulsation' are verbs. 'Hopi, you see, actually has a classification of events (or linguistic isolates) by duration type, something strange to our modes of thought' (p. 215).

These are clearly much more important differences than the lexical ones. To the Greeks, such as Democritus (fifth century B.C.), 'atoms' were minute solid particles. They existed, permanently, and thus were represented by nouns; secondarily they did or suffered actions, expressed in verbs. It took over 2,000 years for scientists to break away from this idea of solidity and permanence, and to regard them as energy, as a process. In Hopi, however, they would have been represented by verbs. Might it be that if this had been the case in S.A.E. the long scientific process of discovery would have been considerably shortened? This is, of course, mere – but perhaps not idle – speculation.

We may use Whorf's words to sum up his hypothesis:

We are thus introduced to a new principle of relativity, which holds that all observers are not led by the same physical evidence to the same picture of the universe, unless their linguistic backgrounds are similar, or can in some way be calibrated. . . . That modern Chinese or Turkish scientists describe the world in the same terms as Western scientists, means, of course, only that they have taken over the entire Western system of rationalisations, not that they have corroborated that system from their native powers of observation (p. 214).

The contrary view is that all languages enable man to discover essentially the same reality, but some parts of it more easily than others: language being a factor, but not the all-important factor, in the process. At the moment there seems little evidence either way.

What is, however, important for our purposes is not so much the ultimate proof or otherwise of the hypothesis, but the emphasis Whorf lays on the way language *habitually* channels our thought. For a variety of reasons this process is of central concern to the teacher and education.

4. SUMMARY

Thought is possible without words, but not to an advanced level. By means of words we develop concepts which enable us to organize our experience, and in one sense to create the world we live in. Poets and writers have been fascinated by the 'world of innocence' which young children create out of their inexperience; and they offer us a view of it complementary to that of the psychologists. Linguists have also been concerned with the way different language speakers may be led to different pictures of the universe, and the *habitual* ways of thinking about it that this implies.

CHAPTER V

THE LANGUAGE ENVIRONMENT

1. *CONDITIONS OF ORACY*

Let us imagine we can select the conditions which would produce the most advanced linguistic development in a child of five. Certainly the child would as a prerequisite have to be of above average intelligence; there is a correlation between intelligence and language development (McCarthy, 1954). However, here we have seen that language is closely related to thought; and, particularly in the pre-school child, it is difficult to measure the one without to some extent measuring the other. For the elementary-school child, in fact, it is accepted that vocabulary is the best single indicator of intelligence. Loban, for instance (1963, p. 87), finds in his large-scale study that the highest single correlation is between vocabulary and intelligence, as measured by the Kuhlmann-Andersen group test of intelligence. There are also non-linguistic intelligence tests for both pre-school and school children, but we have to accept that, in our society, 'verbal intelligence' is at a premium. We no longer regard intelligence as a fixed quantity; *within limits* we may speak of the capacity to acquire intelligence; and the major means of doing this is through language. (Recent tests of language and 'psycholinguistic ability' in young children are Kirk, 1966; Reynell, 1969; Weschsler, 1967.)

Leaving this aside, then, the reader may like to try to give his own answers to the following, in pursuing the question: what ingredients go into the production of a linguistically developed child of five?

(i) What 'political' system: authoritarian/democratic
(ii) What nationality: English/Australian/Irish/other

(iii) What social organization: family/community
(iv) What class: lower/higher
(v) What siblings: none/twins/many
(vi) What sex: male/female
(vii) What language: one/more than one
(viii) What eyesight: blind/seeing
(ix) What hearing: deaf/hearing

We do not know the answers to the first two questions. It would in fact be impossible to do any satisfactory research into them. They are listed here because they obviously must have some bearing.

1.1 'POLITICAL' SYSTEM

An autocratic regime is not concerned to encourage people to talk and to express themselves. Conventional army practice is to require 'Permission to speak, sir' when addressing an officer. It has also been argued by the present writer (1965) that the long tradition of authoritarian teaching in education has resulted in grave limitations on the oracy of the students. Authoritarian methods of teaching have been found to discourage talk and participation in discussion (Lippit and White, 1958; Ryans, 1961).

1.2 NATIONALITY

The nationality of the speaker – if, for instance, we are thinking only of those major countries where English is the first language – has doubtless some influence also. If environment is an important factor in language development, as is clearly the case, then the national culture is part of this. The Irish believe themselves to have the gift of the blarney, though there seems to be no objective evidence for this. A Scottish Inspector reports that Scottish children are probably held back by a national stereotype of 'dourness' (Rankin, 1970). Such matters must have their influence, though it is not really possible to agree on their relative importance.

1.3 SOCIAL ORGANIZATION

On the matter of social organization, however, there is a great deal of objective evidence. McCarthy summarizes studies which show the effects of institutionalization, as in orphanages, on children's language (1954). Moore (1947) compares the speech content of orphanage and non-orphanage children, to the latter's advantage. Goldfarb (1943, 1945) studied the language of children who had spent their first three years in an institution, and compared their subsequent progress at stages into adolescence with that of children who had spent those years in foster homes. The former were retarded both in language and conceptual ability. The lack of stimulation they received at a critical time seems to have been the principal factor.

1.4 SOCIAL CLASS

On the matter of social class there is a large literature. As McCarthy (1954), summarizing the research, says, considerable evidence in the literature indicates that there exists a marked relationship between socio-economic status of the family and the child's linguistic development. Her own research (1930) found that children from higher-status families used longer sentences and more mature sentence forms at earlier ages. Templin (1957) studied the oral vocabulary and structures of 480 children between three and eight, and found that they were superior in higher-status children. Loban (1963), in his investigation of 388 children, found more complex grammatical structures in the higher-status children. As we have seen, Bernstein roots restricted and elaborated codes in the working and middle classes respectively. The work of Labov (1964) on 'dialect' helps us to understand something of the social effects of environment on language. In the U.S.A. the problem of 'dialect' is a much greater one than in the U.K. In the U.K. 'dialect' refers primarily to one of the dying regional forms of tion of the standard language. (See Ch. I, 2.3.1, 2.3.2) In the English, of which the principal legacy is regional pronuncia-

U.S.A. 'dialect' refers to the varying forms of the language (pronunciation, grammar, lexis), often influenced by the original language of immigrant groups, which are to be found in large cities. Some of these may be equated with restricted codes; but at any rate they carry social penalties as against the prestige standard English. Labov asks: 'Why is it that young people, who are exposed to the Standard English of their teachers for ten or twelve years still cannot use this form of speech no matter how badly they need it?' (p. 78) As a result of his work in New York, Labov suggests that new language habits suffer interference from the vernacular, as is the case with the Puerto Ricans. But much more important, he feels, is the conflict of value systems involved; to accept a language is to accept the values it symbolizes: 'many elements of language (certainly not all) are imbued with non-cognitive values as well, and the total information conveyed in these non-cognitive functions may outweigh the cognitive information. Identification with the class of people that includes one's friends and family is a powerful factor in explaining linguistic behaviour' (p. 94). In other words, for some children, to change one's language is to change one's identity. And this may present such a threat to their security as to be unacceptable; conversely, the individual may feel he would be betraying his family or class by changing.

1.5 SIBLINGS

The only child is popularly considered to be 'marred' or 'spoilt'. There seems to be no evidence for this. On the other hand, there is evidence for his superior linguistic development as compared with that of siblings. This was found, for instance, by Davis (1937). Higgenbotham (1961) found that only children gave longer talks, used longer sentences, spoke more slowly, were clearer in articulation than were siblings. Again, twins and triplets are in popular mythology considered a blessing. They are certainly not blessed in language compared with 'singletons', as Day (1932), using eighty pairs of twins, and Davies have shown (1937). (A singleton is a child born singly, i.e. not from a multiple birth.) Triplets seem to be even more retarded than twins (Howard, 1946). The Dionne quintuplets were found to be sixteen to eighteen months retarded at age five (Blatz, Fletcher, and Mason, 1937).

1.6 Sex

It may be disturbing to the male ego to discover that girls have a slight but definite advantage judging by linguistic measures. In the study by Davis (1937) previously referred to, where the subjects talked about were avowedly of interest to boys rather than girls, the girls none the less proved superior. 'In nearly every phase of language studied girls were found to retain up to the nine-and-a-half year level the superiority which has been previously demonstrated for the pre-school period. This is true of articulation, word usage, and length, complexity and grammatical correctness of sentences. Girls use more personal pronouns than boys, and less slang.' Numerous other studies provide confirmatory evidence (see McCarthy, 1954). An interesting recent comment is provided by the finding that adolescent girls taking external examinations in English, in the U.K., obtain higher grades than boys (Jackson, 1969).

1.7 Second Language

This problem takes several forms. We have the case of immigrants to a country who have to learn its language. We have that of a country whose people are turning away from the national language in favour of another, and whose government is anxious to encourage the national language. Again, there is the country which teaches a second language as part of the education of its pupils. In the third case much less time is normally given to the second than to the first language, and it is not the language used for instruction. In the other two cases, however, both languages seem to suffer. Surveying the available research, and drawing also on his own study, MacNamara (1966) finds evidence that the linguistic and educational attainments of bilinguals are inferior to those of monoglots. They tend to develop less well in both languages. He suggests four reasons for this:

1. Linguistic interference from the first language – e.g., certain grammatical forms may persist, certain pronunciations may be used, certain sounds in the second language may not even be heard because they do not occur in the first language. If the languages are unrelated (e.g. English and Chinese) the interference is greater.

2. Cultural interference. The second language may imply an approach to reality different from that of the first (see the discussion of Whorf in Ch. IV, 3). It may not be merely a matter of learning a new language, but rather of learning to see reality through the eyes of a native speaker of that language. (Again, cultures far apart are likely to produce greater problems.)

3. Parental confusion in language. The parents of bilinguals may themselves have learned imperfectly the second language (this applies particularly to adult immigrants), and thus provide poor models of both for their children.

4. It takes *time* to learn a language. If bilingual children learn two languages in the time monoglot children learn one, then both their languages suffer. When one of the languages is not the language of use and advancement, but is taught for cultural and national reasons, then the motivation for learning it may be low, and this aggravates the problem.

It seems clear that learning a second language imposes a burden on development in both languages and on educational attainment. If, on the other hand, it is felt desirable to learn another language, then on the whole the earlier this can begin the better, the problems involved being taken into account and compensated for. In the strictly controlled educational environment of a good home or school, often with able children, this is done almost automatically. But so many of the bilinguals involved are culturally deprived in any case, and the means do not exist for compensation. If good performance in the second language is a social educational necessity, as with immigrants to a country who intend to make their life there, obviously it is the duty of educators to persist with it. If, however, it is imposed for nationalistic reasons, it is likely to become one more burden, and the justifications for doing so need examining very carefully indeed.

1.8 BLINDNESS

It is sometimes suggested that blind children have an advantage over sighted children in their greater linguistic capability. Thus Miller, speculating on the 'most precocious child orator', would have her to be a blind girl (Miller, 1951, p. 158). And it does appear that some blind children talk more than their sighted peers. Thus Maxfield (1936), examining two groups of blind pre-school children (group 1, mean age three years four months; group two, mean age five years eight months), reports: 'Taken as a group the blind children asked many more questions than did the seeing, and gave fewer commands. . . .' It seems reasonable to assume that the totally blind pre-school child is satisfying his need for a feeling of security through talking a great deal, asking many questions, and using proper names frequently.' It is when we come to examine the nature of what is said that the superiority of sighted children is noted. Although the blind do not lag behind in the acquisition of syntax (Tillman and Williams, 1968), 'their verbal abilities focus on a basic vocabulary without much elaboration' (Tillman, 1967). More than this, however, they suffer from *verbalism*, that is to say they are lacking the experience to which the words and concepts refer, to which, as Harley (1963) puts it, 'they can attach insufficient experiential relations'.

1.9 DEAFNESS

The blind child's deficiencies are obvious, and every attempt is made to communicate with him through the medium of words. The deaf child's plight is graver from this point of view. His defect may not be diagnosed for some years, though the situation in advanced Western countries is now better than it was. The deaf child's problem is first and foremost that he does not hear the language he needs. As much as other children he will utter a stream of noises, but the parents will not be able to reinforce for him the significant sounds in the language, and carry out the other strategies, which, as we saw, are essential features of language acquisition. And again, whereas a hearing child, having acquired a new word, will meet it again and again in a variety of contexts, the deaf child will have to have it specially reinforced if he is to make it his own. His ability to conceptualize, to express his thoughts and feelings in words, to organize his life by means of words, will be strictly limited. And thus we find deaf children falling behind in educational attainment and social maturity (see Lewis, 1968). Early diagnosis, the amplification by mechanical means of whatever hearing the child has, and specialized teaching method, are essential, if he is not to fall progressively behind his more fortunate peers.

2. THE CHILD-ADULT DIALOGUE

The factors we have discussed help to make situations that are favourable, or unfavourable, to language development. Do they have a common element which we may say is the fundamental fact in them all? It seems that they do; this element is provided by the presence and language behaviour of an adult. With the young child this adult is in the nature of things likely to be his mother: his intelligence will be developed or depressed by her activities.

It is the mother who will (i) provide the authoritarian or tolerant climate in the home, (ii) embody the national cultural assumptions, (iii) be present in the home, absent in the institution, (iv) talk to the child according to her social pattern, (v) talk to her child more if he is an only child than if he has many siblings, (vi) be the model for for a young girl more than her husband (usually absent) is for a young boy, (vii) help or confuse the child with second-language learning, if this applies,

(viii) give special attention to the blind child. That the 'good' mother provides many essentials for the young child (bodily warmth, security, love, stimulation, etc.) goes without saying. We shall assume all this, and concentrate on her function in providing the conditions for language development and for the 'acquisition' of intelligence.

Let us say at once that the fundamental fact in language development seems to be the nature of the child-adult dialogue. The way children are talked to by adults, particularly by their parents, and even more particularly by their mothers, in large measure determines, for good or ill, their linguistic growth. Brothers and sisters, other children, obviously do have some effect; but the evidence is clearly in favour of the dominance of the adult influence. McCarthy (1930) found the response of pre-school children talking to adults to be of a length superior to that elicited when talking to other children. M. E. Smith (1935) found pre-school children used longer sentences and more advanced patterns of language when they were conversing with adults than those they used with other children. Basically, the linguistically competent adult can 'stretch' the child's language in a way that his peers cannot.

In the past it seems likely that the adult role has been insufficiently appreciated. Consider the actual learning of the native language in the first place. Scholars bow in wonder, stressing the ease, the rapidity, the almost magical nature of this. Chomsky and Miller (1963, pp. 275–6) write:

How an untutored child can so quickly attain full mastery of a language poses a challenging problem for learning theorists. With diligence, of course, an intelligent adult can use a traditional grammar and a dictionary to develop some degree of mastery of a new language; but a young child gains perfect mastery with incomparably greater ease and without explicit instruction. Careful instruction and precise programming of reinforcement contingencies do not seem necessary. Mere exposure for a remarkably short period is apparently all that is required for a normal child to develop the competence of a native speaker.

However, there are far too many children who have 'mere exposure' to language, and whom we consider deprived; and it may well be that when language development is poor it is because there has been either no language teaching going on, or the wrong sort; when it is good there has been the right sort of language teaching.

We have spoken of the role of the linguistically competent mother in the child's language growth. It may be that the variety of ways in which she talks to her child, her 'strategies', represent very skilled teaching indeed, not consciously thought out, but (in measure at least) remembered from the way she was talked to as a child by *her* mother, who in the same way remembered how she was talked to, and so on. It may be that here we have a body of traditional wisdom and practice passed on. We have already glanced, in Chapter III, at some of the strategies of the mother. The mother's language is the model, and that the 'good' mother is consciously or unconsciously aware of this is indicated by the way she often speaks simple distinct well-formed sentences to her child. With the child's own language she does several things: notably, seizing upon sounds in his stream of babble and reinforcing them (it is thus *not* bad practice to accept 'baby' words like *dada, moo, baa,* and so on); and, a little later, expanding his own telegraphic contractions in a variety of transformations. Her early teaching is particularly concerned with supplying nouns and verbs by giving names to things and actions, by naming the objects, or, for instance, by giving a running commentary ('Now let's put your hand through the sleeve'). And there is direct instruction requiring response ('It's a *ball*. What is it?' 'Say bye bye'). One very common device is to require prediction. ('This is the –? What brick are you putting on the –? If you – (please.)) There seems to have been no sustained study made of the teaching strategies of the mother, and it would be very useful to have one.

On the language learning of young children Bernstein's work is seminal. He argues that in the 'working-class home' experience is not 'mediated' through words: that is to say that the child there is not required to express his thoughts and feelings in words to the same degree as in the 'middle-class' home. Affection may be expressed by a hug rather than by 'I love you'; reprimand by a slap rather than by 'You ought not to pull pussy's tail, because it hurts her'. This (manufactured) example also illustrates another fundamental point of Bernstein's; that the working-class mother may use imperatives rather than explanations, partly because she lacks the language to explain and does not herself feel the need of explanations. Bernstein's famous example (1961) is of the two mothers and their respective children on a bus. Both say 'Hold on tight'. When asked why, the one mother says, in effect, 'Because you'll be thrown forward if you don't', and the other 'Because I say so'. The one is teaching the language of explanation and extending the child's curiosity. The other, with her resort to authority, is doing neither.

We have looked at young children's language in the light of the *uses* it may serve. Let us now look at it from another point of view – that of the personal development of the child. Psychologists often speak of this development under three aspects: the conative – connected with the will; the cognitive – connected with the mind; and the affective – connected with the emotions. It will be convenient to use these categories.

3. LANGUAGE: CONATIVE, AFFECTIVE, COGNITIVE

3.1 CONATIVE USES OF LANGUAGE

The child uses language to make his own needs known, to influence others, to gain his ends, to make it clear that he matters. One of the chief ways he learns this is by experiencing the control of his mother over him. However, as we have seen, there is control by request and explanations, and there is control by edict. Teaching is thus going on in social registers at a very early age. Apparently trivial devices, such as requiring the child to say 'please', distinguish between commands and requests, and are thus important in the 'control' of others.

Another way in which conative uses of language are taught is by asking the child to require someone else to carry out an action: 'Go and ask daddy if he will bring in some butter when he comes home, or 'Will you please tell John tea's ready?' Through such teaching something of sensitivity to other people is learned, or not learned.

3.2 AFFECTIVE USES OF LANGUAGE

The language in which feelings are expressed is prepared for in the relationship between mother and child where the mother recognizes that feelings are important, does not deny expressions of affection either way, nor deal with negative feelings merely by telling the child to be quiet.

As the child acquires language his mother will introduce him to the rich heritage of songs, poems, and rhymes which can be found in such a collection as that of the Opies (1951): first the knee and finger games, and later the longer verses. It is clear that the anonymous authors of these pieces understood children, their need for enjoyment and language learning. Some verses help with naming, others with the alphabet; rhymes help with phonemic discriminations, and with a sense of the rhythms of the language; there are built-in opportunities for practice in the refrains and repetitions – as in 'Old Mother Hubbard', 'This is the House that Jack Built'. The classic children's stories also contain similar features – 'Henny Penny' and 'The Three Little Pigs', for example.

The child's mother will not only read the stories and play the language games with the child but will also ask him to say a nursery rhyme to her, to tell her a story. This may be one the child has met, or it may be original. In Chapter VII, 3.6 below we quote examples of children's spontaneous creations. The one beginning 'Lump goes that teddy' has the rhythms of a knee game, and takes a spontaneous delight in ringing the changes on rhyme and assonance: *teddy/telly/teddy/shake shake hands/shake cake cans*, and so on. One need not labour the value of this for reading.

The language the child produces for these purposes will

have characteristics different from that used for other purposes. As we have seen, research indicates that conversation
with adults tends to produce more complex structures. The
reader may like to compare the following 'poem', given in
response to the invitation 'Right, now, let's have a poem/tell
me a poem', with the second dialogue in Chapter VI, 4.1. Both
involve the same child at the same age (three-and-a-half):

right
one day I said to a little pony who was
              in the field over a fence
I'm not going to bang you I'm only going to ride on you
I said shut the door and I'll ride on you
I haven't got a door said the horse
this is really a tease game
am never going to ask you to take me a ride again
so off they went down the lane to
bambury horse cross
they brought a white horse home
they didn't know where their home was
so – (*a wasp interrupts*)
Oh dear what's this bizz bizz go-on stoop
and there was a little girl who says
hallo flower there you are
and that's end of the story daddy.

The qualities displayed in each recording are different. In
the one just quoted there is less control, less complexity : the
girl has to give a free narrative rather than to conduct a discussion. Both are necessary, but each requires a different adult
strategy, to produce on the one hand affective, on the other
cognitive, language. We shall now go on to look at this last.

3.3 COGNITIVE USES OF LANGUAGE

Some functions of the adult in extending the language of the
child as a means for thinking can be seen in the dialogues recorded in Chapter VII. In these there are requirements from
the child in addition to those we have looked at above.

Requests for information
(a) Requiring simple answer: 'Where is that?'
(b) Requiring extended answer: 'And what about –?' 'What else was there?'
(c) Requiring speculation: 'What are you going to be when you grow up?'

Requests for greater accuracy about information supplied
'What's that?' 'What sort of –?' 'Where is –?'

Requests for explanations
'Why is she having some new ones . . .?'
'Why do you want it to go faster?'

Requests for definitions and analogies
'What's the garage like?'
'What's a butterfly?'
'What's a train sound like?'
'What do mummys do?'

It is clear that the adult's function here is to elicit greater information, greater accuracy, greater rationality, greater awareness of relationships.

There has been little investigation of the child-adult dialogue in this connection. However, Hess and Shipman (1965) have argued that the child's style of response to problem-solving situations can be associated with the mother's ability to use verbal concepts in her interaction with him. 160 Negro mothers were asked to teach simple tasks to their own four-year-old children – grouping plastic toys by colours and function, for instance. The middle-class mothers produced more words, used more abstractions and more complex structures; were less likely to be dogmatic, more likely to explain in words than to demonstrate in actions; more likely to provide information for problem solving, to plan and thus to avoid error, to praise. The differences in the mothers were reflected in their children's performances. The workers conclude that the use of language rather than the absence of language is the root of the matter: 'the meaning of deprivation is a deprivation of meaning.'

In a review of the research that exists Freeberg and Payne (1967) found a relation between parental practices and the broad level of cognitive skill. Blank and Solomon (1968) see deprivation as lying not in a lack of stimulating experience but in the 'lack of a symbolic system by which to organize (it)'. Thus an enrichment of the total environment of the child is not likely to remedy the key defects. They see the problem as follows:

Certain types of language, such as labelling circumscribed objects (e.g. bottle, table, ball), can be grasped easily through illustrations and/or imitation. Therefore, no great effort is required to learn these words. By contrast words referring to properties which are not immediately evident require much elaboration for understanding. For example, a word such as 'top' is much more abstract than a word such as 'book'. The word 'top' can refer to such physically different things as the 'top' of one's head, the 'top' of one's desk, and the 'top' of a building. The word unites these instances only when there is an understanding that 'top' refers to the highest point on anything, regardless of how different the 'anything' looks. Other examples requiring a similar level of abstraction are time (before, after), direction (underneath, between), relative judgments (warmer, heavier). It is here that an articulate person, be it mother, teacher or sibling, is required to offer the necessary corroboration or negation of the child's emerging ideas.

This type of feedback is readily available in the middle-class home but is rare in the lower-class home. We therefore propose that this lack of an ongoing elaborated dialogue is the major experiential deficit of the deprived child.

The researchers took twenty-two children (3.3 to 4.7) over four months and divided them into four matched groups. All groups were given interesting inexpensive materials (art materials, toys, books) to enrich their environment, and the teachers showed warmth and interest in what the children did; but in two of the groups there was no attempt at tutoring, the children following activities of their choice. In the other two groups the children were talked to, one group five times per week for fifteen-twenty minutes, the other the same three times per week. With these groups the tutors conducted conversation that required the children to seek information from their own experience, not necessarily that which was immediately present.

The tutors guided the conversations — the children were encouraged, for instance, to speculate ('Where would the doll be if it fell off the table?'); to reason ('What is the weather like today?' 'Can we go and play today?'); to classify ('What foods aren't fruits?'); to follow sequence of thought (the steps by which material can be altered); to verbalize — silently before speaking, or aloud before acting; to become aware of possessing language ('Now *you* tell *me* what to draw'). The tutored groups made much greater gains than the untutored, judged by the Stanford-Binet Intelligence Test, but it seemed to the experimenters that much more important (dramatic) were behavioural changes — the apparent joy in learning, and the feeling of mastery on the part of the tutored groups, in contrast to the non-tutored groups, who displayed none of these attitudes.

The discouraging thing about such 'intervention' programmes is that the effects seem to die away after the experiment has finished and the children revert to their usual environment. However, this study is valuable, both in its diagnosis of the deficiences, and in its classification of the main types of language which it sees the middle- as distinct from the working-class mother employing.

4. THE COMPULSORY SITUATION

One learns language by being in a situation that calls language forth: by being in a particular type of situation that calls forth a particular type of language. Earlier in this book we discussed a model of the 'communications situation', and we saw in it the various factors which combine to produce language.

In this chapter we have been concentrating on the Addressor's influence on the Addressee – the adult's, and particularly the mother's, influence on the child. The 'good' mother has all kinds of linguistic requirements of the child which he *must* fulfil, and which develop him conatively, affectively, cognitively. But to say *must* is to leave the wrong emphasis; he must fulfil them certainly, but he wants to do so, delights in doing so. In that he is required to speak, the situation binds him; in that he can make choice from his increasing mastery of, from his increasing awareness of, the possibilities of language, he is free. It is in this sense that we may define the compulsory situation which is the basis of language learning (Wilkinson, 1969).

It is important to emphasize that language development takes place under *guidance* in compulsory situations. Sheer 'exposure' to language is insufficient. It may appear to work with many children, because the home has in fact provided that guidance and compulsion. When we consider culturally underprivileged children the situation is different. In a devastating criticism of American nursery school provision Bereiter and Engelmann (1966, p. 26) comment:

Indeed anyone familiar with the more unstructured approaches to pre-school education for disadvantaged children is probably aware that more time is devoted to learning about sheep, fire engines, supermarkets, guinea pigs, hair ribbons, freight trains, and simple impedimenta than is devoted to such elementary necessities as learning the meaning of *or*.

There are certain differences between English and American nursery schools; nevertheless, it seems that the criticism may have point in both countries. Bereiter and Engelmann define certain 'minimum goals' in language development in the pre-school as being essential for future progress (pp. 48–9).

Among such goals are:

1. Ability to use both affirmative and *not* statements in reply to the question, 'What is this?': 'This is a ball', 'This is not a book.'

4. Ability to use the following prepositions correctly in statements describing arrangement of objects – *on, in, under, over, between*: 'Where is the pencil?' 'The pencil is under the book.'

6. Ability to perform simple *if – then* deductions. The child is presented a diagram containing big squares and little squares. All the big squares are red, but the little squares are of various other colours: 'If the square is big, what do you know about it?' 'It's red.'

8. Ability to use *or* in simple deductions: 'If the square is little, then it is not red. What else do you know about it?' 'It's blue or yellow.'

11. Ability to count objects correctly up to ten.

12. Ability to recognize and name the vowels and at least fifteen consonants.

'Exposure', it is argued, may give the content words, but not their relationships, expressed in the structure words. Bereiter and Engelmann proceed to teach the skills by intensive formal techniques resembling foreign language drills and repetition, in regular periods of fifteen–twenty minutes daily over six weeks. They claim success in the accomplishment of the goals. They do not claim success in all-round development, but this was not their aim; they can say that such development is likely to take place more rapidly, now that certain linguistic skills have been acquired. There are other American experiments based on Kirk's analysis for the Illinois list of Psycholinguistic Abilities (1966).

Many teachers will find these means unattractive; and they may be right in rejecting them. But Bereiter and Engelmann have at least defined their objectives; they have recognized that teaching as well as learning goes on in this period; and that further learning is dependent on children's having developed a certain schematization which is able to cope with it. Whilst current work in oracy may be adequate for many children in infant school, it seems that the culturally under-privileged are not being placed in the compulsory situations that require verbalization of the right order. And, of course, infant school is a little late for those children who need a nursery school to compensate for the linguistic limitations of the home.

5. *SUMMARY*

Children are more likely to develop well in their native language if they are brought up in a middle-class family, with few or no siblings, under an enabling rather than authoritarian discipline, and with no second-language interference. Girls are rather more advanced than boys. Crucial in their develop-ment seems to be the nature of the dialogue the child conducts with adults, usually the mother. In such a family the language of intellect, will, and emotion, is naturally encouraged: it seems that the children need only be exposed to experience for this to happen. However, investigations with deprived children suggest that mere exposure is not enough; in the middle-class home a good deal of covert teaching goes on, in a 'compulsory' situation, which prepares the child for future learning.

CHAPTER VI

CAPABILITIES IN LANGUAGE

1. *THE LANGUAGE ARTS*

We may classify the language arts, or 'communication skills' as follows:

PRODUCTION RECEPTION

ORACY	SPEAKING	LISTENING
LITERACY	WRITING	READING

It is commonly assumed that there is such a thing as 'language ability': that all four language skills will correlate highly with one another. This is of course a generalization – there are people who speak fluently but write badly, who write fluently but speak poorly, who listen well but express themselves badly; and so on. Nevertheless, the belief may hold as a generalization. But it might be true at certain stages of development and not others; true for young children, not for adults. Again, *groups* of skills seem to be involved in each of these language arts; we might find that the ability to write a report correlates highly with ability to listen, but to write an imaginative essay does not. Or to make the point another way, the instruments (tests etc.) constructed to measure these skills may not be valid.

There is a further problem when a person has the ability to perform well in all the language arts, but never displays it. This brings us to the distinction between Competence and

Performance made by Chomsky (1965), often referred to nowadays. 'Competence' we may define as the possession of vocabulary and grammar, and the potential ability to use them; 'Performance' may be defined as the use actually made of Competence. Obviously, we can never actually measure Competence, because we can only observe it through Performance. The distinction is a simple one, and many examples come to mind. For instance, a man may speak badly in an interview because the situation causes him to be inhibited; a school child appears poor at written composition until he gets a subject or a teacher which really inspires him; and so on. It might be, to return to our main argument, that Performance in, say, three out of four of the language arts does not correlate with that in the fourth because of such inhibiting factors, whereas Performance in the fourth most nearly represents true Competence.

For reasons such as these it is difficult to speak firmly about the relationships of the four language arts with one another. Surveying the research, Carroll (1968) concludes: 'It is now pretty certain, however, that there are separate factors for the traditional language modes, that is, reading, writing, speaking and listening.' There is, indeed, some research which finds no relationship.' Martin (1955), reporting a study with five-six-year-olds, concludes: 'There was little indication that the first graders who talked well would succeed in reading or that the poor speaker would have difficulty in it. Some children who were able to write well did poorly in both speaking and reading. Good readers were poor writers.'

However, the majority of studies do not agree with this finding. They seem to support the view that abilities in the four language arts are distinct but overlapping. Thus Spearritt (1962) discerns a separate 'listening comprehension factor', which, however, is closely related to reading comprehension. Various studies by other workers over a long period show us fairly high correlations (between ·5 and ·8) between these two skills (for a review of research see Wilkinson, 1970). A recent study showed correlations of ·75 and ·73, a higher cor-relation than with Intelligence, ·60 (Wilkinson and Stratta,

1970). On common-sense grounds it seems likely that reading and listening will be related, as they are receptive skills.

Studies with young children are of course particularly relevant to the reading problem. Unfortunately, there are few comprehensive researches in existence. One such is Loban's (1963). He took 338 kindergarten children and charted their language growth over a period of seven years, devising a means of measuring it. His general conclusion was that 'reading, writing, listening and speaking, show a positive correlation' (p. 87). He finds ability in oracy a good predictor of reading ability: 'Another inter-relation already apparent at the third grade level is that those subjects who read well by the end of grade three are the subjects who have ranked high in oral language for the kindergarten and the first three years of the study' (p. 69).

In a research in many ways complementary to Loban's, Strickland (1962) made a survey of the language of 575 elementary school children, in order to discover the relation of their own linguistic structures to those in the books used for teaching them to read. We shall refer to this study again; for the moment we may quote one interesting conclusion, which hints at listening comprehension as the basis for achievement in other language arts: 'The structure of children's oral language as measured by the fluency of use of the common structural patterns was more closely related to listening comprehension than to any other variable. Pupils who rated excellent in listening comprehension used the common structural patterns more frequently than did pupils who rated poor' (25: 86–7).

We may summarize by saying that if it is, perhaps, misleading to speak about a single 'language skill', we can nevertheless recognize the interrelationship of speaking, listening, reading, and writing. They may be closer than we think; after all, handling a pen is not a linguistic skill, and yet lack of that skill may easily inhibit the fluency on paper of a good speller. And again, as we have said, our measurements may be at fault. There is at any rate quite sufficient research evidence to justify our paying attention to oracy as a means of developing literacy; and in a wider educational sense there are further good reasons for doing so.

2. MEASURES OF LANGUAGE PRODUCTION

For a period of over fifty years research workers have attempted to measure the language development of children objectively – by classifying and counting certain language features. (A very useful analysis is given by Skull, 1968.) Let us look briefly at some of the common measurements which have been made.

Length
1. Number of words.
2. Mean sentence length.

Variety
3. The number of *different* words.
4. The variety of parts of speech (adjectives and adverbs indicating greater maturity than nouns and verbs).

These two measures should, of course, be calculated in relation to the total words used. Obviously, there is much more likelihood of variety in ten sentences than in two. Thus what is called the 'type-token ratio' is calculated – the number of the words under study (e.g. adjectives) being expressed as a ratio of the total number of words.

5. The use of unusual words. Words not occurring in the basic vocabulary lists, such as Thorndike's, are given a higher scoring.

6. Variety of sentences used – question, statement, exclamation, etc.

Complexity
7. Occurrence of basic sentence patterns, sometimes modified by considering them as 'phonological' or 'communication' units.

8. More complex sentences — using subordinate phrases and clauses, for example. Thus Loban (1963) used a 'weighed index of subordination', giving one point for each dependent clause, two points for a dependent clause within a clause, and a similar type of weighting for other subordinate features. There have also been analyses of the ability to use transformations.

9. Coherence and Completeness. The occurrence of 'mazes' (false starts, muddles).

10. Ability to complete incomplete sentences (drawing on contextual constraints).

If we may generalize the findings of numerous studies (for summaries of the research see McCarthy, 1954, Carroll, 1968), it has been found that in pre-school children language maturity is marked by: greater number of words; greater mean sentence length; greater variety of words and parts of speech; greater use of unusual words; use of varied sentence types; greater complexity of structure; and superior coherence and ability to use constraints.

It will be obvious to the reader that such objective measures should be used with great care. The situations in which language samples are obtained is of the utmost importance (an importance insufficiently realized in the past by many research workers). In some as yet unpublished work by Wilkinson and Stratta (University of Birmingham Oracy Research Unit) subjects giving a commentary scarcely scored on a modified index of subordination, but scored very high reporting a television excerpt. Ideally, one needs to test subjects in several carefully chosen diverse situations. However, it seems that, used with caution, particularly with young children, these objective measures can be of some value.

We may look at one study in detail as an example of this kind of work. Loban (1963) examined the spoken language of 338 elementary school children from Kindergarten to Grade 6 (ages 4–11). The children were interviewed and encouraged to talk on subjects that interested them; they were then given a series of six pictures, asked to discuss what they saw in each picture, and what they thought about it; and the whole was recorded and transcribed. At first level the language was analysed into structures of the basic patterns: Subject–Verb (*George eats*); Subject–Verb–Object (*George eats onions*); Subject–Linking Verb–Predicate Nominative (*Onions are roots*); Subject–Linking Verb–Predicate Adjective (*Onions are good*); Subject–Verb–Inner Object–Object (*George gave John an onion*). At second level such things as the degree of subordination (use of subordinate clauses, etc.) were examined.

The experiment has its limitations. In the first place the single-interview situation strictly limits the type of language that will be produced. There is no way of telling about this, however, from the research report. Again, we are not told about the type of questions the adult asks in the interview. But these can very largely determine the language of the children. To some extent, however, the large scale of the work ameliorates the situation.

Loban finds that in general the differences in structural patterns used by high-scoring and low-scoring groups is negligible (except that the high group uses more of the linking-verb pattern, and the low fewer complete sentences). The order of words in such structural patterns is, of course, fixed: *man eats dog* is different from *dog eats man*. But there are words, phrases, and clauses that we may use to expand the basic structural pattern, which are not necessarily fixed in position; we can add *usually*, or *when he is hungry*, to either of the sentences just quoted, in any position except between verb and object, and make no major difference to the sense. Loban calls these 'movables'. They do reveal difference in performance. The high group use more of them and are more flexible in their use.

Loban also considers the 'fluency' of the subjects. During their first seven years' schooling they spoke more words in each succeeding year, used more 'communication units' (basically 'spoken sentences') with more words in each. During the first four years they had progressively fewer mazes (false starts and muddles in their sentences), but the average number of words in mazes increased for the low group. All subjects showed the same use of the 12,000 most common words (taken from Thorndike and Large). For the next 20,000 the low group had the ascendancy. Only after 33,000 did the high group draw ahead.

Loban's is an attempt to measure language objectively. From that point of view it is very interesting – it seems to indicate that all normal children have the basic structures and a fairly large vocabulary. He recognizes this, saying that 'classification in this research was not intended as a contribution to study of function', but as part of a 'search for techniques which might reveal differences between subjects high and low in language ability. (p. 16). Another large-scale study, often paired with Loban's, is that of Strickland, which finds similarly that 'children at all grades use a wide variety of language patterns' (p. 102). (It should be noted that we are not talking here of severely subnormal children; Graham and Gulliford (1968) have shown that their inadequate structures are related to the limitations of their short-term memory span.) With the vast majority of children the problem would seem not to lie in their lack of language, but in the uses to which they put the language they already have.

3. LANGUAGE RECEPTION

Most of the research referred to so far concerns one part of oracy – oral production, not oral reception. However, we say in Chapter III that understanding precedes use, and thus it is important for us to look at the skill people exhibit in oral reception.

It is covenient to think of this from four aspects:

1. Recognition.
2. Use of constraints.
3. Organization.
4. Understanding.

3.1 RECOGNITION

It is clear that to understand words it is necessary to recognize them. The basic difficulty we have in listening to a foreign language with which we have no acquaintance is that we do not recognize the words. The problem has been thought about much more in connection with reading, where such terms as 'sight-recognition' are commonly used; but it is no less a problem in listening. We shall take this as so obvious that it does not need further development at this stage, and we shall leave our main treatment of it until we come to discuss reading.

3.2 USE OF CONSTRAINTS

Recognition is of individual words or common phrases (*nice day, how d'y-do, how d'y-do*, for instance). But we must, of course, relate words to one another in the form of phrases or whole sentences. Take the words *going grass train green same lately*: we recognise each individual word, but all together they mean nothing to us. They are nonsense, they do not 'add up'. We have expectations which are being frustrated.

Let us look at this matter in more detail, as it is very important. Whenever, in ordinary conversation for instance, we hear one word, our expectations are aroused about the next one. Take for instance the word *bananas*. We are able to make three sorts of inferences about what will come next. We may call these syntatic, semantic, and phonological.

3.2.1 *Syntactic Constraints*

The syntax of a sentence is the arrangement of its words according to long-established usage (see Chapter I, 3.3). If *bananas* is the first word of a sentence, our expectations, derived from our knowledge of the syntax of English, will be that, since *bananas* occurs early in the sentence, and since it is a noun, it is highly probable that it will be followed by a verb — *bananas are*, or *bananas cost*, for instance. It is unlikely to be followed by an adjective (*bananas rotten*), as the adjective in

English usually precedes the noun; it is unlikely to be followed by an adverb (*bananas slowly*). However, it is important to note that these remarks only apply to the word as used early in a sentence; if it were used late, such combinations would be quite possible (*She called the shopkeeper's bananas rotten* or *The sanitary inspector ate his bananas slowly*).

3.2.2   Semantic Constraints

Semantics is the science of meaning. We have expectations about what words will occur, not only from the syntax but also from the meaning of the words before us.

To return to our bananas. A sentence beginning with the word is likely to continue with a statement about bananas which is within expectation. *Bananas are — yellow, — good to eat, — my favourite fruit.* We are not likely to get *Bananas are — red, — good to write with, — my favourite cannibals —* statements which are surprising, improbable, and impossible. A statement like *Bananas are my favourite fruit* is fairly predictable; a statement like *Bananas are my favourite cannibals* is not. The first is very easy to grasp; if we heard or read the second, we should wonder if we had misheard, or if there was a misprint in the book.

We are considerably helped in listening and reading by the fact that certain things are likely to be said and that other things are seldom or never likely to be said. Sometimes the same idea is expressed in the same words so often that they become a formula: *eggs and bacon, how are you, knife and fork*. Proverbs it is often unnecessary to complete: *a stitch in time . . . we say; too many cooks. . . .* A humorous effect can be produced by frustrating expectation: *He never lets his left hand know what his other left hand is doing.* Often words occur near together without forming formulas. We call this tendency of words to occur in the same context 'collocation'. Thus in a conversation about clocks, while we should not be surprised at words like *strike, hour, finger, spring*, and *weights*, we should at words like *wig, powder puff, corsets*, or *stockings*.

3.2.3   *Phonological Constraints*

If we read aloud a piece of written English, we infer from the earlier words how subsequent and concluding words will be pronounced. In the sentence just finished the *If* that begins it raises certain expectations about word groupings which prevent us giving a concluding note to the word *English* – for there is more to follow. Were the word *If* underlined, to give special emphasis to the conditionality of the utterance, it would preclude our stressing also the *we* (in contrast to *them*), because it is not normal practice to have two main stresses occurring together. Of course, the intonation is linked to meaning and syntax: in the sentence under discussion, we group words in intonation patterns according to the constraints imposed by these two. Certain words in certain positions are likely to signal certain intonation patterns. Thus *who*, *what*, *how* will often, though not always, signal a rising intonation for a question. However, single words do not carry the intonation they will have in a sentence (and thus a concentration on individual words in learning to read will not help in making the right predictions).

We do not normally read aloud, but it does seem clear that in silent reading we are inwardly drawing on the patterns we have learned in the spoken language. This helps us to group words together, to know which words are significant in reference to others, and so on. Thus in the sentence *What a man says is only a part of what he means* the inward intonation is of assistance in separating *says*/*is* and in giving contrastive stress to *says*/*means*.

3.2.4   *Literal Constraints*

We have already discussed three types of constraints. There is a fourth type which operates with visual rather than oral signals: when, in other words, we read. This, 'literal' constraints, implies the influence of the letters on one another. Thus we could add to *s* and get *sc*, or *sh*, or *sch*, and this would lead to further expectations, *scholar*, or *ship*, or *school*. We could not, however, add and produce *sr* or *sz*, as these combinations do not exist in English. Thus what we have is what Shannon (1949) calls 'transition probability' – any sequence of English letters is followed by a variety of letters with varying frequencies in English usage. It appears that one's speed of reading is affected by the likelihood of occurrence of letters; that is to say by the reader's familiarity with the possible combinations.

3.2.5   *Constraints: Forward and Backward*

The most common form of constraint is predictive – that is to say we anticipate what is to come. However, when we are reading aloud we also glance ahead, using the words after those we are actually pronouncing as a guide. Sometimes, when we are not doing this efficiently enough, we reach the end of a sentence having stressed the words in such a way as to produce the wrong meaning; and we find ourselves re-reading it correctly.

When making inferences forward or backward we are making use of the constraints which words impose upon others around them. We have explained this above, but the reader may confirm it for himself by covering single words in the preceding sentence, and seeing how likely it is that he would be *constrained* by the surrounding words to supply them if they were missing.

Let us examine this matter of constraints in a little more detail. When we are reading, writing, speaking, or listening to a sentence, the possible number of words which could have been used narrows the further we proceed. This may sound a puzzling statement, so we may take such a simple sentence as *The dog gnaws a bone* and examine the decisions the writer of it must take, albeit largely unconsciously. We take the situation of *writing* a sentence, in order to simplify the matter by disregarding all the phonological constraints and concentrating on the semantic and syntactic.

In *The dog gnaws a bone* each word and each combination of words as we proceed acts on the next to restrict our choice of it, as in the diagram. Before we choose the first word, all the words in the English language are open to us: when we have chosen the last word, there are no further choices to make. At each stage from first to last word the choices narrow.

All possible choices open

    1. The
    2. The   dog
    3. The dog   gnaws
    4. The dog gnaws   a
    5. The dog gnaws a   bone
                No further choices needed

There follows a simple analysis of the kind of choices being made; the words/parts of speech given are merely examples of the many acceptable choices which could have been made.

1. All possible choices open; any word and any part of speech.

2. *dog* or *aardvark* (improbable), NOT *as* or *weep* (grammatically unacceptable).

3. *gnaws* or *dances* (improbable), NOT *speaks* (dogs can't) or *mat* (grammatically unacceptable).

4. *the* or *a*, NOT *teach* or *softly* (grammatically unacceptable).

5. *bone* or *slipper*, NOT *man* (who would move rather than be gnawed) or *hopelessly* (grammatically unacceptable). All possible choices made.

3.3 ORGANIZATION

What the constraints help us to do is to organize the words in the sentence into some recognizable form. We may or may not understand what the sentence means while we are doing this. Thus a tired mother may read her child a bedtime story which the child enjoys, without knowing at the end of it what she has read. In this case she is using the syntactic and phonological constraints more than the semantic. On the other hand, if we are to understand what we read, we must have arranged the words into a recognizable form.

Let us pursue in a little more detail this matter of the organization of words that we make. It is a feature of certain games that one is required to arrange words in a meaningful order. Thus, given the words *is February often very in it cold,* we should have no difficulty in rearranging them as *it is often very cold in February).* Here we are making use mainly of semantic constraints. But we may rearrange words without reference to meaning, and know that if the words were meaningful this order would be correct. To illustrate this a simple experiment may be carried out. If the words *gonter, siptless, crailes, a, eadfully* are written on separate pieces of paper and a variety of people asked to arrange them in what they consider the correct order, then the majority will produce (according to an experiment carried out by the writer).

(1) *A siptless gonter crailes eadfully*

Fewer will produce:

(2) *A siptless gonter eadfully crailes*

A few will produce:

(3) *Eadfully siptless crailes a gonter*

All these versions make, grammatically, a well formed sentence. There will also be one or two which do not:

(4) *a crailes gonter eadfully siptless*

Why did the majority produce (1)? Clearly because of their underlying sense of a certain sentence pattern in English into which we slot the words. Sentence (1) accords with what we have called Pattern 2 (Ch. I, 4.2):

(subject)	(intransitive verb)	(optional adverb)
a siptless gonter	crailes	eadfully

Compare

| a zygodactyl | flies | gracefully |

Sentence (2) is of the same pattern, but with verb and adverb reversed: eadfully crailes (cf. gracefully flies).

Sentence (3) is a variation of what is still the same basic pattern, in that subject, intransitive verb, and adverb are present:

eadfully	siptless	crailes	a gonter
desperately	hopeless	flies	the zygodactyl

Compare

There is a further point of importance. Whatever order the words come in, they are still used as the same part of speech. This means that the people arranging them must have recognized this from the words themselves. They could not have done so from the order, because there was no meaningful order when they received the words. They would, for instance, recognize, probably not consciously, that the ending *-less* often marks an adjective, the ending *-fully* often marks an adverb; they would consider it more likely that a verb would be like *crailes* (*fails*, *flails*, *hails*) than like *gonter*. They would also look at the relationships between words: *a* must come somewhere before a noun and not before a verb; *crailes* could of course be a noun, but a singular noun following *a* would not be likely to end in *s*; and if it were a singular noun, and we tried to make *gonter* the verb, we should need the singular form *gonters*; and so on. These processes sound complicated, but in fact any one getting any one of the versions (1) to (3) must have gone through them, and others like them, unconsciously.

3.4 UNDERSTANDING

So far we have spoken of recognition as the fundamental process in listening and reading, contextual constraints being means by which we are helped to recognize words. Now recognition implies that we already know the words we meet, because either we have met them in the spoken language or we have read them elsewhere.

Recognition is, further, a matter of identifying semantic, syntactic, phonological patterns. By the use of the word 'patterns' we intend to imply that the reader has met those kinds of arrangement before, the patterns are independent of the actual words. Thus the reader has certainly met all the individual words in *Mary had a little lamb* before; and he has almost certainly met the whole sentence before. On the other hand, it is unlikely that he has met *Gary had a pickled ham* before, because the present writer has just made it up. Nevertheless, the pattern is perfectly familiar to him.

There is of course a further problem – whether the reader not only recognizes the words but can relate them one to another, so as to 'understand' the whole group, sentence, or paragraph they constitute. This is not only a language problem. It involves a thinking process, of which the explanation is imperfectly understood. Basically, however, it seems to be as follows. The world of the infant is full of actors, whom he learns to label: *Mummy, Daddy, dinner, drink, egg.* These actors perform certain actions: *Daddy go,* or have certain actions done to them: *want drink.* In other words, he sees enacted before his eyes the connections between words. His mental development partly consists in abstracting these words from objects present before him (thinking of them when they are absent), and later on being able, by *analogy*, to think of non-concrete things in the same way. What is laid down in the 'mimes' he witnesses in early childhood is a sense of relationships between objects, and these are represented by words. The difference between *Mary has a little lamb* and *Mankind has a great potentiality for good* lies in the degree of abstraction. Our thinking processes are basically those we saw enacted in that theatre of early childhood.

4. LANGUAGE SKILLS IN YOUNG CHILDREN

In this section we shall look again at the linguistic skills discussed above. It might seem to the reader of this book that these are fairly sophisticated and not likely to be possessed by young children of normal ability. However, this is emphatically not the case, as we hope to demonstrate. Let us take the two skills already discussed in general, and discuss them in relation to such children. These skills are the ability to organize and the ability to make use of constraints.

4.1 ORGANIZATION

By the age of three-and-a-half or four most children have mastered the basic structures of their language, in that they use them; the basic sentence patterns are there and most of the transformations can be operated, as Menyuk (1964) and Slobin (1966), for instance, established. Menyuk even found that nearly all the basic syntactic structures could be found in upper-middle-class children as early as two years ten months (1963). (For other relevant research see Noell (1953), Strickland (1962) and Loban (1963)). This does not, of course, mean that if children are brought up with a non-standard English, such as a Negro dialect of New York or a dialect influenced by Creole in the West Indies, they will acquire the structures of the standard form. For the present purpose we shall assume we are discussing children learning the standard form.

Here are some sentences produced by a boy of two years eleven months in conversation with an adult:

1. I done some painting.
2. *Have you done some painting at school?*
3. I've done some painting on the painting book.
4. *What does it do?* (*Discussing toy lion.*)
5. It doesn't do anything.
6. *What sort of a noise does it make?*
7. It doesn't make a noise.
8. (*Volunteers*) I did give some flowers to my mother.
9. *Where did you get the flowers from?*
10. From the tray I did get it from.
11. (*Referring to spools on tape-recorder*) I want it to go faster.
12. *Why do you want it to go faster?*
13. Because I want it to.

14. *What have you got in your pocket?*
15. I've got lots of some money in my pocket.

These are no unacceptable forms in structure; even the second part of line 10 is rather the result of an afterthought than a doubt about order. The subject-verb-object pattern is handled with confidence (1, 2, 8), with the addition also of adverbial phrases (3, 8), and even a subordinate noun complement (11). The boy can transform the adult's affirmative questions into negatives (5 from 4, 7 from 6). His accidence is behind his syntax (a point we anticipated in Chapter III); he is uncertain about the simple past, and uses *did* acceptably (8) and unacceptably (1) (the unacceptable form was not used by the parents). However, he has clearly met the form with *have*, and seems to have been reminded of it by the adult (2), for he uses it in 3, having had, however, to make a difficult transformation. The use side by side of acceptable and unacceptable forms of accidence is common in learning; contrast, for instance, the use of *some* in 15 and 8.

Children develop language rapidly. Here is a conversation with a girl of three years five months, asked to talk about her imaginary (girl) companion Sweetheart.

1. All right. Now for gin with we want to know all about Sweetheart's Mummy and Daddy. Now, this is the tune of it. Now, this is the tune of it, Now, this is the tune of it. (*Sings*) Da da da da
   Can we go to Bunting?
   No we can *not*.
   Now I want you to tell me where Sweetheart lives.

2. Well she lives here because her Mummy — her old Mummy and Daddy are not coming back.
   Where are Sweetheart's Mummy and Daddy?

3. They're at the doctor's so for having some new ones from Father Christmas
   Why is she having some new ones from Father Christmas?

4. Well because her old ones are dead.
   Won't they get better?
   No, I'm afraid not.
   What's the matter with them?
   Well they've got bad backs.
   Where did you say Sweetheart lives?

5. Well she lives here because her old Mummy and Daddy
   are very late.
   Is Sweetheart here now?
   Yes, she's lissing – listening to this tape recorder.
   I can't see her.

6. Well if she's hiding under David's white cricket stand, we
   know.
   I've lifted it up look, but I can't see her.
   (*Laughs*) She's there look!
   I can't see her.
   You can!

This utterance exhibits several interesting features. The
girl is handling the adverb clause of reason not as a formula
but as a free utterance; she places three different explanations
within the same structure (2, 4, 5); she uses a result clause correctly (3), and apparently a conditional clause (6). What hap-
pened in this last case, however, was that she came to the pause
represented by the second comma, and hesitated before finishing rather lamely with 'we know'. To her the utterance did
not make sense, but she had embarked upon a pattern signalled
to her by 'if' and felt compelled to conclude it.

This certainty of the syntactic structure as against the un-
certainty of the semantic is common. It arises because children
learn the syntactic patterns from a limited set of words, and
then have to apply these patterns to new words they meet.
Accidence now seems to be as acceptable as syntax. The overriding urge to communicate and the pressure of the syntax
cause her to substitute where she cannot call up a word rather

than have the utterance fail: *for gin with* (1), *for instead of she* (3), *stand instead of sweater* (6).

4.2   USE OF CONSTRAINTS

We have spoken about various types of constraints. In practice we probably make use of several at any one time rather than a single one. In addition the whole situation is important.

Let us look at this matter of the total situation as it affects young children. Here is a further short piece of conversation with the same girl of three years five months as in the previous section. She has heard fairy stories about a good queen and a bad queen, and in fact identifies with the former.

> *And what about the queen's mummy?*
> Oh I haven't got one. I don't need one.
> *You don't need one. I see.*
> Do I?
> *Do you need a daddy?*
> Yes of course to give me my food of course don't I?
> *And what about David, about your brother David?*
> Well I have him.
> *I see.*
> He's ill at the moment. He he's not in bed.
> *Are you the good queen?*
> Yes.
> *What about the bad queen?*
> Oh she's died. She's died of naughtiness.

The interesting thing to note here is that the girl usually gives *explanations* with her answers, though these are not asked for. She is, in other words, predicting from the total situation, and from previous situations like it, that she will be asked for them, or at least that they are necessary.

In the following example there is not simply a general expectation of the possible requirements of the adult, but a specific supplying of his words:

Where will you go to?
Mm, to the village.
Yes.
What to buy?
Yes. Where else would you go to?
To er to coffee.

The girl gives what ought to have been the next question, which the adult has failed to give or to respond to.

5. SUMMARY

We may discern a difference between Competence and Performance in the language arts, between the possession of language and the use actually made of it. It seems that abilities in the four arts, speaking, listening, reading, and writing, are distinct but closely interrelated. A good deal of work has been done on measuring children's language production, and the findings are encouraging. Basic Competence appears nearly always to be present, but there is often a failure to realize it in Performance.

The skills of language reception are recognition, use of constraints, organizing, and understanding; and we have demonstrated how these are present in young children.

CHAPTER VII

THE DEVELOPMENT OF ORACY

1. *LINGUISTIC DISADVANTAGE: ITS NATURE*

As we saw in Chapter VI, the evidence accumulates that the large majority of children have a basic Competence in language, not necessarily realized in Performance, and that this is acquired comparatively early. This means that they can operate the grammar of their language, and possess a vocabulary, which may be surprisingly large, upon which to operate it. Children commonly called 'linguistically deprived' or 'linguistically disadvantaged' have this Competence. Let us consider the nature of this disadvantage.

1.1 *'Poor English'*

The first reaction of the intelligent layman if we asked him to define 'poor English' might be to say 'bad grammar'. Perhaps he might have in mind those obsessions of the purist, the split-infinitive, 'it's me', and so on; but more probably he would mean simple and common deviations from accepted forms, such as the confusion of number between subject and verb (*we was, I were*, etc.). These are some of the chief indicators of what our layman might call 'illiterate speech', and they often damn a speaker. The interesting thing, in view of this, is how comparatively trivial they are against the total grammar the speaker is using correctly. They are rarely causes of misunderstanding, which would certainly be the case if the total grammar were at fault. From work by Loban (1966) it seems likely that most mistakes made by children occur in fifteen common irregular verbs; that mistakes with *be, have* and *do* account for most of these; and further, that the mistakes are mainly of two kinds only – disagreement of subject and verb, and confusion of the two forms of the past tense (*I done it*, instead of *I did it*, or *I have done it*).

A second comment the layman might offer in defining poor English might be 'poor vocabulary'. We usually find, however, that the linguistically disadvantaged child has words to carry on the communication required of him at home or in the playground. It is when different things are required of him in a different situation, such as the school, that his vocabulary will seem to be inadequate. And yet it is not necessarily sheer numbers of words that he lacks; some such children talk a good deal. It is something to do with the quality and variety of the words he uses.

On reflection, the layman might also say that someone's English is 'all right' when he is talking to friends, but otherwise he doesn't seem to be able to manage very well. His English is restricted in use. A fourth comment the layman would almost certainly make would be about the accent or pronunciation he associates with poor English.

Now all four of these – grammar, vocabulary, restricted use, and pronunciation – have something to do with linguistic disadvantage, but in a deeper sense than the layman realizes. In what sense will become clearer when we have looked at some of the studies made in recent years.

1.2 RESTRICTED CODE

In a series of thought-provoking papers Bernstein refers to all four (1958, 1959, 1961, 1962a, 1962b, 1964, 1969a, 1969b, 1970). He calls disadvantaged language, which he identifies with that of the lower working class, a Restricted Code. It is restricted in the sense that it can be used in, for example, the home or the gang, but it is not adequate or acceptable in other circumstances. In contrast he calls advantaged language an Elaborated Code; it is a language in which advanced thought is possible, it is sensitive and flexible. Bernstein several times (1958, 1959, 1961) lists the linguistic differences between the two codes; and the following classification draws on these lists, together with other information from his writings:

		Restricted	Elaborated
Sentences		shorter	longer
		grammatically simpler	grammatically more complex
		unfinished	finished
		loose syntax	controlled syntax
		acceptable forms	unacceptable forms
		few subordinations (phrases, clauses, etc.)	more subordinations (phrases, clauses, etc.)
		use of short commands and questions	requests and explanations of various kinds
Parts of speech	verbs	active	active and passive
		simple verbs (*destroy*)	complex verbs (*will have been destroyed*)
		rigid and limited	flexible and varied
	adjectives and adverbs	few	more (e.g. '*one* would think', '*it* seems likely')
	impersonal pronouns		
	prepositions	common and repetitive (*and, but, so, because*)	including logical relations (*if, unless, whether*)
Collocations		idiom and cliché from stock	less resort to these; more individual choice
Relevance and coherence		less	more

	Restricted	Elaborated
Abstraction	less	more
—Centric sequence	socio-centric (phrases like *you know, see*)	ego-centric (phrases like *I think, I suppose*)
Meaning	implicit (i.e. the language states it generally)	explicit (the speaker knows what he means and can find exact words)
Feeling	rather communicates attitude: often by phonological means (e.g. loudness)	communicates fact and logic: attitude is implicit

It will be seen that the characteristics are rather mixed — linguistic (grammatical and phonological), psychological, sociological. Here follow two manufactured examples in which the reader might like to try to discern some of the characteristics of each code:

(a) So me and Mike goes down to the museum/cause we had to didn't we/and we gets there/and we sees these dirty big statues all Greek and that/know what I mean/like at Euston there was a statue there in the caff/

(b) So Mike and I went down to the museum to see if we could get some ideas for our project/and when we got there we saw these large marble statues/I think it's considered they're mainly Roman copies of Greek originals/

These useful distinctions between much 'good' and 'bad' English will probably receive considerable assent from the reader. But Bernstein goes further. He speaks of the two codes as bringing about, and being brought about by, some fundamental psychological differences in children. A restricted-code speaker, asked to cope with the language and thinking tasks of a school, will be at a great disadvantage compared with an elaborated-code speaker. 'For the latter it is a situation of linguistic development whilst for the former it is one of *linguistic change. . . .* This is by no means to say that a (restricted-code) speaker cannot learn. He can, but it tends to be mechanical learning, and once the stimuli cease to be regularly reinforced there is a high probability of the pupil's forgetting. In a sense, it is as if the learning never really gets inside to become integrated into pre-existing schemata' (1961, p. 175).

However, subsequent experiments, particularly those of Lawton and Hawkins (1969), fail to confirm any differences of the absolute kind suggested. For instance, in one experiment Lawton required teenaged working-class boys to discuss a fairly abstract topic, and their language suggested 'that they can be made to use something which is at least approaching an Elaborated Code' (1968, p. 143). And in his latest published paper (1969b) Bernstein himself has abandoned the original rigid division: 'because a code is restricted . . . it does not mean that the children cannot produce at any time elaborated speech in particular contexts.'

Coulthard (1969) commends the tremendous impetus for research which the Restricted/Elaborated Code model has provided over the past decade, but in a critique of Bernstein's work does not find the model meaningful, and suggests that a new formulation is necessary. And in fact the very old formulation has led many to think fatalistically of two types of children; in the members of one 'backwardness' has been so 'culturally induced' that they appear to be almost a different breed of animal. The position, however, seems to be that many restricted-code children have a Competence which can be called forth in an elaborated Performance if the situation is right. Bernstein (1970) is inclined to accept the gloss on his work given in Halliday (1969) that it is rather in the range of *uses* to which language is put than in any particular linguistic features that we may find restriction or otherwise. Halliday, as we shall see below (section 3), offers a horizontal model. Bernstein's is essentially vertical; models of both kinds are therefore needed if we are to say something about *levels* of use.

1.3   *The Root of the Disadvantage*

If we cannot in the last resort define language disadvantage in linguistic terms, we can nevertheless agree about its existence. This, therefore, is the problem: if children have the basic linguistic equipment, why is it not used and developed by many of them? The answers must be complex and varied, but ultimately they come down to a matter of motivation; such children do not feel the need to do so. Now by 'need' here we do not mean anything the individual is aware of or can speak about, but a deep unconscious feeling of the worthwhileness or otherwise of doing something.

The root of the disadvantage of many people is that they do not feel a *need* to develop their language, and the reason is that they are unaware of the possibilities of language. They imperfectly appreciate the nature, the uses, and the joy of language. They have a jewel which is worth a fortune, which can be worked to a rare edge of precision, which can be cut to a many-faceted beauty; and they are playing marbles with it in the backyard.

How adequate, then, are the layman's views of 'poor English' that we looked at at the beginning of this section? They are useful as far as they go, in that poor vocabulary, poor grammar, ability to speak only in a restricted situation, and poor pronunciation are often marks of disadvantage. Pronunciation, for instance, may be so wide of the standard, because of regional or dialect variations, or bad articulation, that it is a barrier to our understanding; or even if it is not it may carry social penalties (see Ch. I, 2.3). But if we take a more fundamental view, these things are but symptoms of a deeper failure to realize a basic Competence in Performance.

2. *THE POSSIBILITIES OF LANGUAGE*

Clearly, we wish to encourage an awareness of the possibilities of language in children. By 'awareness' we do not mean that the children will be able to put into words these possibilities; rather that they may know intuitively some of the things language is and does. And this awareness goes hand in hand with their *use* of language, for without the first we cannot have the second. Let us take these two kinds of awareness in turn: what language is, and what it does.

2.1   AWARENESS OF WHAT LANGUAGE IS

Language is a *series of signals* to which meanings are arbitrarily attached (see Ch. I, 1); but in order that these meanings shall add up to meaning, the signals (words) must be arranged in order; they must be *patterned*. Now, as we have seen, some meanings and some patterns are more likely than others. This point and this kind of awareness have been discussed in detail already. Our awareness of possible meanings and patterns is important in our *reception* of language; it is equally important in our *production* of language. And we derive this awareness from our experience of language; of hearing it, and of using it. The type of language-experience the learner has is crucial.

Our relationship with language is of two kinds, bound and free. If we speak a language we are normally bound by its grammar and vocabulary. To use one part of speech for another to any extent would be to become incomprehensible. But for special reasons a part of speech is sometimes changed. Shakespeare uses a pronoun as a noun:

Lady you are the cruelest she alive.

The advertiser uses a verb as a noun because he feels this gives more impact than a noun like 'necessity':

For you this is a must.

It is normally the semantic aspect of language, however, and not the grammatical in which we have most freedom. We can use the grammar and vocabulary to say anything we can think of. In many situations we are bound to say things one way rather than another by the social conventions: *How do you do?*, for instance, when being introduced, not *How are you?*, which requires a different answer. Much conversation, apparently free, contains a large number of set expressions of the order of *Nice little place you've got here*, *Well I ought to be off*. But even if the expressions are not there, the same type of thing is being said; or as we put it nowadays, the same language 'strategies' are being employed. A teacher with a class will probably have fixed expressions for class control: *Get on with your work*, *Get your exercise books out*, *Turn to page (three)*; but the strategy she uses, requiring the children to read a passage and answer questions on it, for instance, may have a linguistic form varying between one occasion and the next. In this case she feels herself bound by the strategy (it would be ridiculous to answer the questions *before* reading the passage), but free with the words.

It is characteristic of some people, such as comedians and poets, to frustrate our semantic expectations for their own particular ends. The poet who writes:

She found his diary deep in dates
His soul she scorched, his book she burned:
'I'll make it up my love,' he wept
– And over a new fig-leaf turned.

is using our knowledge of the phrase 'to turn over a new leaf' to frustrate our expectations of it. Such expectations are equally strong in young children, as anyone who has tried reading to them 'Mary had a little pig' knows only too well.

Language, then, is a series of choices; and the awareness we are speaking of is an awareness of these, of what is likely to be said, of what is less likely to be said, of what is unlikely but possible to say. This knowledge is not conscious, but intuitive with the native speaker. There are different ways of saying the 'same' thing; within a register, in different registers, some common, some less common, many unique. There are the main roads, the secondary roads, the individual's own route. When we *produce* language we not only make the main decision of direction, but are constantly making decisions along the way, our possible paths getting fewer as we are near our destination. When we *receive* language we are using our knowledge of possible routes to travel with the speaker. Of course our expectations often go beyond the words used: we may be paying attention to the covert meaning, to the intention of the speaker, of which he may be unaware. The little girl mentioned in Chapter VI (4.2) is making an assessment of meaning going beyond the words to the whole situation.

2.2 AWARENESS OF WHAT LANGUAGE DOES

Language is behaviour. This phrase is often used to stress that it is essential a part of man's activity as walking or eating. In fact, one of its main functions is to supplant physical behaviour. It cannot replace eating; but through modern aids such as the telephone it can save us a walk to give a message.

Let us look at certain kinds of physical behaviour in order to discover the way language has supplanted and improved on them. Let us imagine a Non-linguistic Man, who makes no noises whatsoever. He lives in a tribe with other Non-linguistic Men, Non-linguistic Women, and Non-linguistic Children. They will have long hair and go naked like characters in a modern film or stage play. Let us imagine also a correspond- ing group of Linguistic People. Let us imagine Non-linguistic Man taking certain actions; and compare them with the words of Linguistic Man.

Non-linguistic Man	*Linguistic Man*
1. Grabs food.	Requests/demands food.
2. Pushes child away.	Orders child to go.
3. Huddles with others, grooming and touching each other.	Converses with others on topics of common interest.

4. Contemplates his navel; Uses words to explain himself to himself and others.
   studies his reflection.
5. Explores the jungle. Asks questions about the world; formulates his understanding in words.

6. Dances to represent the Tells a story; writes a poem.
   hunt or war.
7. Shows an object to others. Uses words to describe an object, happening, or idea to others.

It will be immediately apparent how crude is the communication of Non-linguistic Man compared with that of Linguistic Man. The former cannot, for instance, communicate about an object which is not present (7); the latter can. The former can only communicate broad meanings, not shades of meaning.

3. *MODELS OF LANGUAGE USE*

In many ways the young child in the first eighteen months of life is very similar to Non-linguistic Man; between the ages of eighteen months and four years he develops into Linguistic Child. He develops the awareness that language can serve various functions formerly served by various physical means. Halliday (1969) has suggested seven uses of language of which the child has knowledge, the seven of Linguistic Man. As he says, 'The child knows what Language is because he knows what language does.'

Let us therefore examine the language of a three-year-old child, using Halliday's headings of use, or 'models'. All the examples are recordings of the same little girl between three years five months and four years of age.

3.1 INSTRUMENTAL MODEL

This is the use of language for satisfying material needs. It will be remembered that the eighteen-month-old child of our Chapter III used such language as *want dinner, want down now.* The three-year-old is beginning to learn that there is more than one way of making the demand:

daddy / can I have / can I have a chocky?
if you . . .
if you please / daddy.

3.2   REGULATORY MODEL

In a sense the girl just quoted is not only satisfying her own needs – she is requiring someone else to do something for her. She is 'regulating', 'manipulating' the behaviour of someone else. Children experience this use of language frequently from *Drink your milk* and *Don't pull pussy's tail* to *Get out your exercise book.* And of course they employ it themselves.

3.3   INTERACTIONAL MODEL

Again, language is used between people in their interactions, in close personal and less close relationships. It has many functions in conversation, from small talk on the one hand to serious discussion or intimate interchange on the other. It shows a sense of other persons, and of oneself in relation to them. Thus it may define and consolidate the group. Almost any conversation can be used to demon᷏ this use of language:

what are you going to be when you grow up?
I don't know / I must be a a / I'll be a washer up / a j / a
jobber / I'll be
a jobber / what's that /
you know / don't you / work

The 'you know / don't you' exhibits a prior knowledge of the adult, and of his role as 'all-knower', together with a slight but definite hint (in the recording) that he is being distanced ('why ask questions to which you know the answer?').

3.4   PERSONAL MODEL

By language the child discovers and makes public his own individuality. He begins to understand himself and his relation to others, to express his feelings and attitudes towards things and people. A simple statement, *I love you*, is at once a statement about self, and of the position of self towards someone else.

An excellent example of the little girl using role-playing to discover more about herself occurs in the following conversation, where questions and statements about 'the queen' become questions and statements about herself.

/*I want you to tell me about the queen* /*where does the queen live?*
in her big palace.
in a big palace /*and where is that?* /
at 27 Elm Road.
at 27 Elm Road /*I see . . . .* /*and what about the queen's mummy?*
/*oh* /*I haven't got one* /*I don't need one.*
you don't need one /*I see.*
/*do I?* (*Rather anxiously*)
do you need a daddy?
yes of course /*to give me my food of course don't I?* (*Certain of this*).

The girl is attempting to determine her own place in her basic human relationships with her parents.

3.5 HEURISTIC MODEL

The word 'heuristic' is from a Greek word meaning 'to discover'. We are thus concerned here with language as a means of finding out, particularly about the external world. The child seeks facts and explanations:

what else was there in the old days?
I don't know /*how* /*how did they get* /*how did they* /*daddy*
yes
how did /– *how did they get plants and things like that* /
they must have grown them /*what sort of things did they have in the old days* /

they had black and white houses/didn't they/

yes

well how did they/well they had/did they get wirelesses
daddy?/

The little girl is using language to discover not only facts but
their explanations (*how did they get plants*); she is using
language not merely to discover but to confirm what she is
not quite sure of (*they had black and white houses/didn't
they*). Of course children of this age are quite able to supply
explanations; they may not be correct scientifically (see for
example the recordings quoted in section 4 below), but they
are provisional explanations, useful at a particular stage in
development. Others are perfectly logical:

what's the garage like?

To keep things in to keep the car in so that it won't get wet
from the rain.

3.6 IMAGINATIVE MODEL

It seems that young children have a natural feeling for rhymes,
rhythms, melodic sequences. This might seem a hazardous
statement to make – it could be argued that they learn this
from an environment which attaches great importance to these
things. On the other hand, we have seen the way that the
baby described by Weir (Ch. III, 3.2) seemed to rehearse and
repeat syllables and phrases in a patterned way for the sheer
joy of so doing. Still, there is no doubt that the environment in which the child is brought up has a good deal of
influence.

The little girl whom we are quoting provides an instance:
by three-and-a-half she had had a good deal of experience of
songs, poems, and nursery rhymes, and when asked to tell a
poem would make up spontaneous and strongly rhythmic
sequences sung to tunes. The two following as printed give
only a dim impression of the joy and charm of the recordings:

well, let's have a poem about a swing then
yes all right
swing swing swing/round and round the wind carries me/
the wind carried me, wind carries me/who told me/oh my
daddy told me/dum dum dum dum dum dum/here comes
Tim/here comes Tim/here comes Tim/walkity walk

This next is partly based on the baby knee-riding game, where
the one adult knee with a child on it races the other:

lump goes that teddy/lump goes that telly/lump goes that
teddy/that was the wrong knee/lump goes that telly/lump
goes that teddy/lump goes that telly/lump goes that telly,
with that little nobby/ring ring that bell/shake it/shake
it/shake it/ring ring that bell/knock knock/knock knock/
wock knock knock knock/shake shake hands/shake shake cans/clap clap/clap clap clap/dan dan dan/
hake cake cans/clap clap/clap clap clap/dan dan dan/
wasn't that lovely?

In contrast, here is the opening of a spontaneous recorded
story:

one day/one day Joseph said let's go and see if we can see
Jesus anywhere/so they opened the door and broke it/do
you know what they did then/Mary said what's that moving
there I don't know let's go and see/so they went over and
tapped it and a little eye came up/eek/who's that/he said/
it's me/now we've found you for goodness sake come back
with us/at once

And this is a complete story, which gets sidetracked first by a
bird in the garden and then by a pen on the desk, but which
reveals the girl's sense of an artistic whole by returning without prompting to conclude the story of the little pig:

once upon a time/there was a little piggy/he walked along
the road and he/sneezed/suddenly he thought/oh I've got

a cold/oh dash I'll go and get I'll go and get home/and get a
coat on/oh dear I'll go and see the doctor and get some
medicine/oh dear (. . . . .) so off he went back home/
don't he said/no hat he said/and it blew right away over
the/south coast/oh blow that hat I'll run and catch it run
fast run fast run fast/that's better said the pig/I've got it
now/it hasn't blown very far has it/no/what's that he said/
nothing/bird/no/a thing/that's right/no that's a pen/no
it isn't/a pen can't talk/don't be stupid/yes it can/no it can't
now (. . . . .) well he went home and he got a coat and put
a nice warm hat on on top of his other one then he went
out again/oh/the doctor was coming down the lane/oh
blow he would know whether I've got a cold wouldn't he/
so/he went back home/and he got there before the doctor
did/that's it/

3·7 REPRESENTATIONAL MODEL

Language is a means of conveying messages — passing information, for example. Many adults tend to think of this as the first,
perhaps the dominant, function of language; but it is interesting that we have been able to list six uses of language by the
child without mentioning it until now. Nevertheless, it is
certainly an important function of language.

what does (a policeman) look like?
he looks like/he's got grey trousers with a black hat on and
he's grown up/he has white gloves on
that's very good/now what about the postman?
he/he arranges the letters and gives them to people
yes/and what do mummies do?
do the work
yes/I see
they didn't have mm/they did have buses didn't they
yes
with with horses and carts
what sort of buses?
don't know

what used to pull the buses?

the horse and cart (*tone meaning 'it's so obvious'*)

4. MODELS: VERTICAL AND HORIZONTAL

The way of classifying children's language which we have just looked at is only one way of classifying it. It is, we might say, a horizontal classification. That is to say it lays out before us some types of language; but it does not say anything about how well or how badly children use them. For instance, it will not tell us how to judge whether the poem of child A is better than the poem of child B. In other words, it has no vertical dimension (and is not intended to have any).

To make the point by examples let us quote a few answers of the three–four-year-old girl in the last section; and give after each the answer given to the same question by the same girl at the age of eleven (in both cases the answers are spoken straight into the microphone).

What's a butterfly?

1. it's a / butterfly bun /
2. a butterfly is an insect / which normally has many bright colours /

What's a train sound like?

1. / ch, ch, ch, ch. ..
2. the old fashioned steam ones used to / sound like chuff / but the modern ones have a whistle and / rumble along rather like a bus /

What's the garage like?

1. to keep things in / to keep the car in so that it won't get wet from the rain.
2. it's a wooden building / painted white / with two large doors and / three windows

1. nice/
2. it's a long object which has an engine at the front and in the old days/they used to have steam/and the train is used for carrying people from station to station/and place to place

Since in some fashion even Non-linguistic Man is aware of all seven models, as we saw, it is highly probable that all children except the very severely disadvantaged have the same awareness as applied to language. And the girl, at both ages, has this awareness in general terms. But obviously her linguistic abilities have developed considerably. When younger she is not capable of the two tasks of defining and describing required by the questions, as she is when older. Her answer to question 3 comes nearest, but is really an answer to a question which wasn't asked. Her answer to the question *What's a butterfly?* retreats from an attempt at definition, and substitutes a phrase using the same word, but probably without any idea of the visual analogy intended by it; the answer she gives when she is older, however, is well on the way to being a complete objective definition. A classification calling both of these attempts types of Representational Language is horizontal; a classification that in some sense said the older was 'better' than the other we should call a vertical classification.

We are, however, in difficulties if we try to talk about 'better' language without reference to the basic 'communication situation' we discussed earlier in the book. The girl when younger is communicating adequately according to the requirements of the situation at that time, the expectations of the adult, and her own capabilities. But her older use of language has more general applicability – that is to say it will prove adequate in a wider variety of situations, it is not so restricted.

We need then to consider: the uses of language the child

has; the situations in which we expect these uses; the applicability of the language – whether it is situation-bound; and finally, its appropriateness. In connection with this last we have seen some hints that the girl is developing a sense, not just that she must communicate at all costs, but that there are different ways of communicating the same thing. On one level she realizes that 'please' helps a request; on another she is aware – in the story of the search for Jesus – that adults have a different mode of talking to children. She is aware of registers.

5. SUMMARY

Capability in language we may characterize as an awareness of the possibilities implicit in language:

(i) The child is aware *what language is*, that it consists of choice points at which decisions have to be made, and the greater his awareness the greater his choice. We may recall the child in the previous chapter (VI, 4.2) who makes her choice of what to say on knowledge, not merely of the questions, but of the whole communications situation.

(ii) The child is aware of what language does – it expresses will, mind, heart; or, to put it another way, accomplishes certain tasks for him, and finds out, communicates, and so on.

(iii) In addition, we should say that the child is aware of the *joys of language*. In this book we quote examples of children's delighting in language. There are the pre-sleep dialogues of the child learning languages (Chapter III, 3.2), there are the spontaneous stories, poems, and songs of the 3-year-old (3.6 above), there is the joy of accurate definition in the 11-year-old (4 above). The deep and unconscious delight in language is one of the marks of difference between advantage and deprivation; the deprived child is deprived of joy.

CHAPTER VIII

THE BEGINNINGS OF READING

1. *FACTORS IN READING*

1.1 INTRODUCTION

We saw in Chapter III that understanding of language precedes its production. The common practice of teaching reading before writing would therefore seem to be soundly based, leaving aside the greater mechanical difficulties of writing (see, however, Chapter IX, section 3.2). It is beyond the scope of this book to discuss writing: for the remainder of it we shall concentrate on this next of the language arts to be acquired, reading.

It will be clear from the whole argument so far that the language environment in which the child grows is of fundamental importance for his language development in both oracy and literacy. This we shall take for granted now, and return later. For the moment let us look at what research shows about some of the other factors affecting reading.

1.2 EMOTIONAL FACTORS

Most children by the time they come to reading have made certain adjustments towards school in general. They are eager to learn, able to co-operate with other children, trust their teacher, are glad to accept guidance, can concentrate and persevere for a reasonable time for their age. Such children, if there are no complicating factors such as we shall discuss below, are set fair to learn to read, and indeed to carry out the other learning the school requires. On the other hand, there are occasional children who are emotionally disturbed from an early age. Many severe reading cases are withdrawn, showing shyness, submissiveness, apprehension; a few, however, are aggressive (Robinson, 1949). Anxious restless children may be reading failures (Gregory, 1965); but it seems that with intelligent children, but not with others, anxiety is associated with high reading performance, perhaps because they find in reading a refuge from a world which frightens them (Scarborough, et al, 1961).

The causes of emotional disturbance are obviously many, but are basically centred in the relationship of the young child to his parents. If this is unsatisfactory, or non-existent, then problems develop. The mother may so protect the child that without her he lacks initiative and perseverance (Hattwick & Stowell, 1936), or may set such high standards for him, perhaps as represented by the achievements of his siblings, that he despairs. Sometimes the child's hostile attitudes to his parents are transferred to his teachers, so that he resists any approaches from them; sometimes he copies parental attitudes – a passivity and lack of desire to achieve on the part of his father, for instance (see studies referred to by Vernon (1967)). Of course such emotional disturbances are likely to produce an inhibition of learning in general, not only of reading. Other children who seem fairly normal may for some reason not succeed in learning to read when their fellows do, and thus develop a sense of failure about it which causes emotional troubles and increases the difficulties. It is therefore true to say that one cause of reading failure is reading failure. And since reading is the basis of learning in much school work, the child's all-round backwardness will increase, and his self-concept will be impaired still further. What we conceive ourselves to be and the abilities we conceive ourselves to have are important factors in determining the tasks we undertake and the level of achievement we reach in them.

1.3 INTELLECTUAL FACTORS

Poor readers have on the whole a lower I.Q., as measured by intelligence tests, than have good readers. Malmquist (1958) found the mean I.Q. of his poor readers was 96·62 compared with 107·9 for the whole sample. Obviously the normal verbal reasoning tests are useless in such cases, as they require reading to do them, and oral and picture tests, such as the Terman-Merrill (1960) (L.M. Form), the Merrill-Palmer (Stutsman, 1931), or the Wechsler Intelligence Scale for Children (W.I.S.C.) are preferred, and even these should be used with great caution (see, e.g., Morris (1966), pp. 305–6).

Sub-normal intelligence does not in itself preclude an individual from reading. E.S.N. children will learn to read more slowly than normal children, and obviously will never read difficult material; they can, however, be taught to read at a certain level. Houghton (1967) reports a severely brain-damaged child, with a Terman-Merrill I.Q. of twenty-four, who none the less had some reading; and further investigation discovered other such children with I.Q.s of between twenty-five and fifty who yet could read.

1.4   EDUCATIONAL AND SOCIAL FACTORS

Morris (1966) carried out a survey of ten primary schools in Kent over a period of three years, 1954–7, with certain follow-up studies, looking at 'factors centred in the child' (mental, physical, emotional attributes, attendance and migration); 'factors centred in the home' (socio-economic status, culture and stability of home, size of family, parental help and encouragement, children's reading and other out-of-school activities); and 'factors centred in the school' (class organization, class and reading environment, reading materials, methods and contributions of the teachers). Making allowance for the attributes of the children and the material circumstances in the schools, she concluded that 'each school's success or failure in promoting good reading standards and/or progress depended mainly on the quality of its head and staff in that order' (p. 279). As might be anticipated, in contrast to good readers, poor readers tended to come from homes of lower socio-economic status, with more mothers at work, without books and library membership, with greater numbers in the family, and offering less encouragement to read.

The conclusion that the head and teachers are the dominant factor is interesting. Reading methods, class size and organization, are not so important. Many other researches support this. Southgate (1965, 1966) argues that the overriding factor is the existence of a 'reading drive' in the school. Ramsey (1962, p. 151) compares three methods of teaching reading to sixth-grade children, and concludes: 'Given the good teacher, other factors in teaching and reading tend to pale into insignificance.' This does not mean that some methods are not to be preferred to others, nor that some children do not progress better by some methods than by others.

1.5 PHYSICAL AND PERCEPTUAL FACTORS

Clearly, defects in hearing and sight can limit reading ability. Children with severe hearing loss are likely to be noticed; those with slight loss, which affects their hearing, and thus their recognition and differentiation of certain sounds, may be missed. But even children without hearing loss may not be able to distinguish certain sounds if these are not part of their experience.

Defective eyesight may affect the child's perception of letters, cause strain, lower motivation, and increase anxiety. It is argued that some children have difficulty in controlling their eye movements and thus fixating words, though this is a matter of controversy.

Some backward readers appear to have poorly developed visual perception. They may have difficulty in distinguishing one shape from another, or recognizing the same shape in different positions. Ames and Walker (1964) show that children who subsequently read well give more accurate responses to Rorschach ink-blots than those who are later retarded in reading.

More serious perceptual difficulties are often classed together under the heading 'dyslexia' (i.e. 'displacement of letters') though there is argument about the usefulness of this term (see, e.g., Miles (1967), Houghton (1967)). The condition is sometimes referred to as 'word-blindness', but this is inaccurate

The dyslexic has difficulty with reading and with writing. In reading he will reverse letters, reading *b* for *d*, *p* for *q*; he will change their order; his shape recognition is poor, so that he will misread words, perhaps guessing from context. In writing there will be similar errors – reversals – *het* for *the*, *nda* for *and*, and bizarre spellings which bear little relation to the phonetic form of the word.

It should be emphasized that the very existence of dyslexia as a condition, as distinct from something more than retardation in reading and writing, is disputed. Certainly the concept may be fatalistic; it may lead people to assume a special and incurable state instead of backwardness capable of remedy by educational means.

2 to 6. METHODS OF LEARNING TO READ :

A Note on Terminology

A good deal of confusion is caused by the indiscriminate use of terms like 'method'. Basically there are only two *methods* of reading – through our eyes and through our ears; the former we call 'sight' methods, the latter 'sound' or 'phonic' methods.

The English alphabet is not phonetic; that is to say we find some letters, and some combinations of letters, pronounced differently in different words (*bough, cough*, for example). Thus attempts have been made to help the new reader: for instance, by using a more consistent alphabet, i.e. altering the 'signalling system', the appearance of the words themselves. These are alterations to the *medium* (plural *media*).

There are many reading schemes or programmes in use in schools, consisting of series of graded readers, charts, flash cards, work books, and so on. They are accompanied by a teacher's guide which sets forth the recommended procedure. They may advocate one *method* or another, they may advocate mixed methods; they may or may not adjust the medium. Each usually claims to be a complete programme by which the child may learn to read. We shall call these 'reading schemes'.

We shall discuss *methods* now; and *media* and *schemes* in the next chapter.

2. *SIGHT METHODS*

2.1 WORD WHOLES

It is highly improbable that the reader of this book will so far have come across any word he did not recognize at a glance. It might seem that one way he does this is by taking in the total shape or configuration of the word. The word 'dog' has the shape ⌐⌐, which clearly distinguishes it from 'cat' ⌐⌐ . A few years ago this idea, that we recognize things as a *whole*, fascinated many people. Thus it is often his general appearance that enables us to recognize an acquaintance, though we may not be able to remember details such as the colour of his eyes or the shape of his chin. The *Gestalt* school of psychology offered a theory of perception based on 'Gestalt' or 'shape', and the educationists drew support from this for an approach to reading based on word wholes. In this approach the child learns simple words, not by building them up from individual letters, but by learning to recognize them as complete words.

However, it is only partly true that we recognize things as a whole. It is easy enough to distinguish a short fat man from a tall thin man in this way; but what when there are several short fat men, as might occur in a police identity parade? It is then that the detailed differences become important – colour of eyes, shape of chin, for instance. In the same way, we can distinguish 'dog' ⌐⌐ from 'cat' ⌐⌐ , but when we come to distinguish 'dog' from 'dig' ⌐⌐, or even from 'lip' ⌐⌐, then we are in difficulties. In fact total shape is only one of the visual features of words which enable us to distinguish them; others are clearly the shape and position of individual letters (see Chapter X, 1.2).

The recognition of words by sight, from their configuration and other visual features, is the basis of the 'look-and-say' method of learning to read, which is particularly associated with the name of the American scholar A. I. Gates. By this method the learner is required, as a first step, to acquire what is called a 'sight vocabulary' of a limited number of words that he will meet in his first readers. One such *The Key Words Reading Scheme* (Murray, 1964) requires a sight vocabulary of the following fifteen words to enable the child to tackle the first reader: *a, and, blue, chimney, door, has, house, is, it, my, of, red, roof, the, window*. Words may be taught in a variety of ways. Objects in the classroom may be labelled ('door', 'window'); pictures of other labelled objects may be displayed ('house', 'chimney'); the shapes of the words may be traced; cards with single words — known as 'flash cards' — can be used for recognition. Word-matching and lotto-type games can be played. The learner then proceeds to his first reader, where the words will be used and repeated to familiarize him with them; meanwhile he will be learning by the same techniques words to be used in his second reader; and so on.

2.2   SENTENCE METHOD

The sentence method starts not with individual words but with groups of words and simple sentences. It is argued that the true unit of meaning is not the word but the sentence. Let us illustrate. Take the present sentence. We know the meaning and pronunciation of the words. But let us scramble it: *Present the take sentence; Take the sentence present*. Our first impression may be that the result is nonsense, but as we look we realize that we can in fact make some sort of sense of both. And look what is happening to the word 'present' in the process:

Take the *present* sentence: i.e. the one before us   (adjective)

Present the take sentence: i.e. give   (verb)
(cf. Pass the sweet pickle)

Take the sentence *present*:   i.e. gift   (noun)
(cf. Take the Christmas present)

The three different meanings (and two pronunciations) of the word 'present' which occur in these three sentences illustrate well how closely bound up is the meaning of an individual word with the words around it, and the order in which they are arranged. Thus, it is argued, a child learning by the sentence method will have clues to the nature and meaning of individual words from the rest of the sentence which are denied to someone learning entirely by word wholes.

One common procedure with this method is for the child to dictate to the teacher a sentence of his own, describing (say) a picture: 'The farm is red', for instance, which the teacher will write below the picture. This, and other such sentences, will form the pupil's early reading matter. This is, of course, likely to motivate the pupil well. When reading books are used, such as the *John and Mary Readers* (Ashley, n.d.) and *Adventures in Reading* (Keir, 1951), the teacher does a good deal of reading herself in the early stages, and the child 'reads' by repeating or remembering what he has heard. She will indicate with her finger the whole phrase she is reading and not just the individual word. Thus the first page of Book 1 of the *John and Mary Readers* is:

Once there was
a little boy.
His name was John.
He had a little sister.
Her name was Mary.
John and Mary had
a mother, and father.

By this method the learner is introduced to simple sentences or groups of words, often in association with pictures which bring strong clues to the meaning of the words; and there is repetition of groups of words with slight variations. Thus in one reading scheme (Carver and Stowasser, 1964) we find the sequence, all with labelled illustrations, *three boys on a branch, three boys falling, three boys in a barrel,* where there is a constant and a variable element. Pupils must, of course, look in detail at individual words at some stage, and most writers do not dispute this; but they are concerned to emphasize the advantages of the sentence method as a way of *beginning* reading, because it sets words in a meaningful context and is likely to provide more interest and a greater variety of subject-matter than word-whole and phonic methods.

3. SOUND METHODS

3.1 ALPHABETICAL METHODS

> He that ne'er learns his A, B, C,
> For ever will a Blockhead be;
> But he that learns these letters fair
> Shall have a Coach to take the air.
>
> Anon. (18th cent.) *The New England Primer*

In the eighteenth century, and before, the Alphabetical Method was the usual means of learning to read. The learner used to be taught the names of the letters and had to recognize them by these names. This was the origin of the alphabet books. A famous American example was the *New England Primer*, first published about 1785–90, which contained word examples each beginning with a different letter of the alphabet, and an illustration apiece: A Apple, B Bull, C Cat, and so on. Most examples were animals or birds, the most notable exceptions being Z Zani, and X Xerxes. The tradition of alphabet books survives today in the cheap painting-books for children. It seems to have been common for the letters to be baked in gingerbread. When the child could name the letter he was permitted to eat it. The poet Prior describes it thus:

> To Master John, the English maid
> A hornbook gives of ginger bread,
> And that the child may learn the better
> As he can name, he eats the letter,
> Proceeding thus with vast delight
> He spells and grows from left to right.

This is likely to have been a highly successful method, but unfortunately we have no statistics.

When the pupil had acquired his alphabet he was introduced to words. For each he was required to say the letters and then the word: *bee, ay, tee – bat*, and so on. By this means he memorized the words and the spelling. It may be that such a method would be helpful to the spelling of certain pupils over and above sight-recognition methods. Mr. Squeers of Dotheboys Hall in *Nicholas Nickleby* (Chapter VIII) certainly found it useful:*

This method is not much used today, though in the Kent enquiry Goodacre (1966) found certain experienced teachers using it; and certain modern schemes use a version of it (see Gattegno, Chapter IX, 1.2). No teacher, of course, would deny that children should learn letter names at some stage; it is the naming of letters as a means of learning to read that has fallen into disfavour.

3.2 PHONIC METHODS

In the alphabetical method the letters are given their names, as we have seen. In phonic methods the letters are given their sounds, and the pupil has to blend or run these into one another to make up the pronunciation of the word. This depends on his knowing the word already, for no pronunciation of individual letter sounds builds up exactly into the sound of the whole word. Take a very simple example: *muh-a-tuh* is the nearest we can get with individual letters to the word we pronounce *mat* (to rhyme with *cat*). The child knows *mat* and usually makes an identification between it and the rough approximation he has uttered. This is fortunate, because the letter sounds could equally stand for a non-existent word which we might spell *muratter*. But what when the child does not make the identification? This is one of the limitations of the phonic methods. There are various phonic approaches.

3.2.1 LETTER PHONICS

In this approach individual letters are sounded, and the sounds run together to approximate to the sound of the whole word,

* 'C-l-e-a-n, clean, verb active, to make bright, to scour. W-i-n, win, d-e-r, der, winder, a casement. When the boy knows this out of the book he goes and does it.'

as in the example *mat* given above. This seems to be the most common phonic method. However, it is not without its problems. There are only twenty-six letters in English but these stand for over forty sounds. Thus the letter *a* may represent the differing sounds found in *mat, all, car, bass, ate, any*). The usual way of dealing with this is to introduce the sounds in sequence in the early readers to ensure that the learner understands one way of sounding before proceeding to others.

Some teachers prefer to teach some sounds in combinations. These have come to be known as 'phonograms' (though strictly speaking a phonogram is a symbol for a sound and thus a single letter is a phonogram).

One way is to take the beginning sounds in simple words, e.g. *ma-n, ma-p, ma-d, ma-m*, and teach these. A difficulty comes when words like *ma-r* have a long *a*. However, this is no more and no less a problem than the differing pronunciations of *a*, just mentioned. The objection to this method, that one is teaching sounding habits that will have to be untaught later (Dolch, 1951, p. 201) is wrongly phrased. There is nothing to unlearn, but additional sounding habits to be learned for the same letters.

3·2·2   FINAL PHONOGRAMS

An alternative is to require the learning of the combinations which end words – e.g. the -*it* in *hit, bit, sit, lit, fit*, and so on. Of course single-letter sounding is still required for the initial letters (or for the final letters with initial phonograms), and the child thus has these to learn in addition to a variety of phonograms. Perhaps a more serious objection is that this alternative requires the child to look at the end of a word first. One very important thing he has to learn is that left to right order is essential for reading. If he has to look at the ends of words first, it may confuse him, and lead to his reversing letters and syllables in trying to read them.

3·2·3   THE ORDER OF SOUNDS

If we were writing a conventional phonic reading scheme we

should have to make some decisions about the order in which to introduce the sounds. There are many lists of suggestions for this order. Most lists begin with the consonants as pronounced at the beginnings of words, followed by short vowel sounds; they then come, in varying order, to ending consonants, long vowels, and so on. Dolch makes a justification in psychological terms for the order of the Thirteen Steps he suggests:

THE THIRTEEN STEPS IN LEARNING SOUNDING

1. Sounds of the single consonants.
2. Sounds of the consonant digraphs, *ch*, *sh*, *wh*, *th*, *ck*.
3. Short sounds of the vowels, *a*, *e*, *i*, *o*, *u*.
4. Long sounds of the vowels, *a*, *e*, *i*, *o*, *u*.
5. Final *e* rule for long sound of vowels.
6. Double vowels, *ai*, *ay*, *ee*, *ea*, *oa*.
7. Diphthongs, *oi*, *oy*, *ou*, *ow*, *eu*, *ew*, *oo*.
8. Sounds of vowels with *r* – *ar*, *er*, *ir*, *or*, *ur*.
9. Soft *c* and *g* before *e* and *i*.
10. Taking off prefixes and suffixes.
11. As many syllables as vowels.
12. Divide between two consonants or in front of one.
13. Open syllables long; closed syllables short.

It will be noted that this list does not advise us on which consonants and which vowels to teach first. It is, however, common to introduce letters like *m*, *t*, *b*, *p*, *n* early, and to leave *k*, *q*, *v*, *x*, *y*, *z* till later (e.g., Hildreth (1958)).

4. *VOCABULARY*

The language of this book is too hard for someone learning to read. Its vocabulary is too difficult and its sentence construction too complex. The writers of reading primers are usually very careful to control the vocabulary they use, and to employ simple sentences. It may be that they are overzealous in these directions; but that is a point we can discuss later (see Chapter X, 5). Let us at present concern ourselves with the various ways which have been employed to choose a first reading vocabulary for children.

4.1 WORD COUNTS

Numerous research workers have built up basic word lists – the basic 200, or 500, or 1,000. We may distinguish those which attempt to record (i) what children say, (ii) what they write, (iii) what is written for them in readers, etc. (A very useful summary is given in Burroughs (1957).) Many lists tend to draw from all these sources, from other people's lists, and to some extent from newspapers and books not designed for children: see Thorndike (1944), Gates (1935), McNally and Murray (1962). Because the compilers were not able to use tape-recorders it may be that their lists are short on what children actually say.

We may expect two sorts of words in such lists – content words and structure words (Chapter I, 4.1). We should expect that the same structure words would be common in all lists, because there are comparatively few of them. No matter what the situation may be they are likely to occur. McNally and Murray (1962) found that the twelve most common words in their count were nearly all of this type, and claimed that they accounted for 25 per cent of the words in the reading matter they examined. The words were *a, and, he, I, in, is, it, of, that, the, to, was*; with another twenty similar, they accounted for one third of the words in the reading matter they reviewed. These were *all, as, at, be, but, are, for, had, have, him, his, not, on, one, said, so, they, we, with, you*.

Content words, on the other hand, will vary much more with the circumstances in which they are collected. Burroughs finds that words like *blanc-mange, blue-tit, bird,* and *Jack-in-the-box* occur in his sample, but not in the lists of others he compares them with. He also compares his first 220 words with those of Dolch and finds many differences. There will, of course, be many content words that nearly all children have in common – names of day-to-day objects, the family, and so on. But children's reading matter may be more interesting to them precisely because it does not confine itself to such words.

4.2 Choosing a Basic Vocabulary for Reading

When we have access to basic word counts our problems are not by any means over. Some people would not use them, be-lieving that children will make most progress by reading what they themselves or their fellows have spoken and written (see Chapter IX, 2.3; 3.2). Let us accept for the moment, however, the necessity of some sort of graded reading scheme.

Our choice of words will be determined by the kind of approach we wish to adopt. Consider these three examples – one from a sentence scheme, another from a phonic, and the third from a look-and-say (whole-word). It is not difficult to distinguish them.

(i) Here is another Red Indian. The canoe is on the river.
(ii) The pig in a wig did a jig.
(iii) My house has a red roof.

Obviously a phonic scheme (ii) will pay more attention to the sounds of the letters, introducing new ones gradually, and reinforcing those already learned. In the whole-word scheme (iii) the child will already have built up a basic sight vocabul-ary. Notice how none of the words is the same shape, and how none of them has similar letter combinations (not more than one *oo* or *ou*, for instance). The sentence scheme (i) is not concerned with phonics (it is impossible to build up 'canoe' phonically), nor with shape ('canoe' and 'river' have the same shape), but rather with the context, so that the child may be helped by the meaning of the whole sentence.

Phonic schemes will introduce sounds according to a prin-ciple of order such as that of Dolch (3.2.3 above). Whole-word schemes will take into account the principles of fre-quency in the basic lists. However, as we have seen, the most frequent words are structure words, and, as a glance at the lists of McNally and Murray above will show, whilst it is not impossible to make up sentences from some of these words, such sentences would be so dull as to be useless. In addition, they are not well suited to sight acquisition by the usual methods, because they cannot be illustrated, and because of their similarity in some cases (*in*, *is*, *it*, for instance). Reading schemes employing this method thus often extend their range of content words outside that of the basic lists. Sentence schemes are even more adventurous, with a wider range of content words, relying on the interest of the material to motivate the pupils. All types of scheme will of necessity constantly include and repeat the basic structure words, as it is impossible to write or speak without them.

5. MIXED METHODS

The principal methods of learning to read are the phonic, the word-whole, and the sentence methods. So far we have discussed these as though they were distinct, and indeed one has sometimes been advocated to the exclusion of the others. However, the most common practice is to use a mixture of methods. In a survey of schools in the London area Goodacre (1966, p. 8) found that the majority used a combination of at least two methods, emphasizing particular ones at different stages of a pupil's development. In fact, it is seldom one finds a reading scheme today which is exclusively concerned with one method, though it may emphasize one more than others.

This is sensible, for each technique makes use of a different type of reading skill. The pupil who has built up a basic sight vocabulary gains immediate confidence on finding himself able to read a simple sentence. However, many word shapes are similar, and he may fall into confusing *which* with *whose*, *not* with *now*, and so on. He will need to know what sound the letters stand for if he is to avoid those mistakes, and here phonics may have a place. Even if they are not taught by phonic methods, children who learn to read successfully do acquire indirectly a knowledge of sounds. Another limitation of a strict look-and-say method is that it cannot deal with words not already in the sight vocabulary. In that case a phonic approach to it may be necessary (though not all words can be tackled phonically). The contribution of the sentence method is to place the words to be read in a meaningful relation to one another, so that the other words give clues to the recognition of particular words. 'Once upon a –': most readers will be able to supply 'time'. To be able to do this is an important skill in reading. But used completely alone it can encourage wild guessing. 'Once upon a – (Friday)' requires the reader to do something more than use contextual clues; it requires the ability to distinguish the appearance of 'Friday' and 'time'. Mixed methods are also useful because all children do not do equally well with one method. It is certainly a common experience of teachers that children who are having difficulties with one method often improve if transferred to another.

6. THE PLACE OF METHOD

Which then is the 'best' method of teaching reading?
We have just said that each of the three methods described above is doing a different thing – one teaching the pupil to recognize words by appearance, a second to recognize words by building up their sound, and the third to recognize them by using their context. If this is accepted then it seems pointless to exclude any one in favour of another. Why should the pupil not have all the help which can be offered?

In that case the problem becomes not one of which method to choose, but of which method to use at any particular stage in the child's development. General opinion is that children can acquire a sight vocabulary earlier than they can use phonics. Schonell (1945) speaks of a reading age of seven as being necessary for phonic readiness. Hence phonic methods are least suited to backward readers. This is supported by such work as that of Burt and Lewis (1946). However, it should be said that this is disputed by workers like Diack (1960) and Stott (1964).

However, it is important to emphasize that the *method by which reading is taught is only one of the many factors contributing to the pupil's success or otherwise in learning to read.*

7. SUMMARY

The general factors affecting language development discussed in Chapter V apply to reading (though it also introduces new physical and perceptual problems); we have been looking at some of the research which considers the factors in direct relation to reading.

Turning to the beginnings of reading we find a confusion of terminology between *method, medium,* and *scheme.* Basically there are only two methods of learning to read: by eye, and by ear. It is important to note that method is not all-important: nor are media or schemes. This is a point we shall discuss more fully at the end of the next chapter.

CHAPTER IX

MEDIA AND SCHEMES

1. *MEDIA*

In the previous chapter we have looked at some methods of approaching the printed text. We have not considered the printed text itself, but have assumed that the letters will be the twenty-six of the traditional alphabet which we normally use for reading and writing. We speak of anything written or printed using these letters as being in 'traditional ortho-graphy' (t.o. for short). This is the usual *medium* for reading and writing.

However, there are more sounds in English than there are letters; the result is that a letter may stand for more than one sound, as does the *a* in *bat, car, call, late, any*. A group of letters like *ou* may stand for the sounds in *blouse, coup, bought, touch, cough, could*. On the other hand, one sound may be represented by several different letters or groups: the long *ū* sounds occurs in *flew, blue, coo, two, to, bruise, crude,* as well as in *rheumatism* and *manoeuvre*. This being the case, it has sometimes been felt desirable to modify the orthography so as to make it easier for the pupil who is learning to read. We can do this in three ways:

1. *Diacritical marking.* We can put marks or symbols over ordinary t.o. letters to indicate their pronunciation.

2. *Colour keying.* We can print t.o. letters in different colours; or print them on coloured backgrounds of differing shapes, to indicate their pronunciation.

3. *Simplified spelling.* We can simplify and regularize the spelling of English whilst retaining the t.o. letters. Thus

in Wijk's *Regularized English*, *of* would become *ov*, *is* in Wijk's *Regularized English*, *of* would become *ov*, is *iz*, *was woz*, *many meny*, and so on.

Alternatively, we can give one symbol to each sound. If the t.o. alphabet is used this will necessitate confining its letters to one of their sounds, and supplying new letters for the remaining sounds. The International Phonetic Alphabet uses thirty-eight symbols, of which twenty-two are t.o. letters. Of course a phonetic alphabet might use completely new symbols.

We shall now examine some of these media as employed in the teaching of reading.

1.1   DIACRITICAL MARKING

A brief description of a modern style of diacritical marking in the work of Fry (1964) will illustrate the system. The aim is to mark certain letters so as to give clues to their pronunciation.

1.1.1   FRY

Silent letters are crossed out: 'maïd', and 'madē', for example. Unaccented vowels have a comma over them, as in 'ago' and 'enough'. Long vowels have a bar above them: 'gō', 'mē'. The broad *o* sound is marked with a circumflex: 'ôff', 'auto'. [The scheme is American: in British English a short *o* would normally be used in 'off'.] Two letters standing for one sound (what are called digraphs) have a bar under both letters (c̱ẖat, ṯẖat, s̱ẖut, w̱ẖen, siṉg̱). There are only three consonants that have two sounds, and where the second sound is required the letter has a bar under it (i̱s, g̱em, c̱ity). And so on. Thus a marked text would look like this:

That mòrning a big ôrangē truck cāmē down the strēēt

How successful is such a method of teaching reading? Fry himself conducted an experiment over two years in which he compared children using a standard American reader, *The Sheldon Basal Reader* programme (Allyn and Baker, 1963), in t.o.; children using the same reader with diacritical marks;

and children using an initial-teaching-alphabet scheme, *Early to Read*. The teachers were systematically trained in the three systems, and the decision as to which they used was made by drawing lots. There was no significant difference between the reading ability of the groups after one year, and again after two years.

This experiment shows that the scheme using the diacritical marks was no better than the other two schemes in these circumstances. But it was the general *schemes* that were being compared: it may be that methods of teaching, or the reading matter used (which was the same for only two of the groups), had more influence on the results than the form of the medium. The experimenter himself feels that he may have been attaching too much importance to the medium. He says: 'Possibly we should look for something beside the alphabet as being vital to the efficient acquisition of reading skills. We have a suspicion that that something is teacher ability' (p. 166)

1.2 COLOUR KEYING

1.2.1 'Words in Colour' (Gattegno, 1962)

The basic devic of this scheme is to associate a particular sound with a colour. It does not matter how that sound is spelt. Thus the *e* in *the* has the same sound as the indefinite article or the *a* in *about*, and thus they would all be printed in the same colour, dark yellow.

The scheme is phonic. The author has analysed the language into forty-one sounds, and these sounds are printed in colours on wall charts. The teacher begins with the vowels, first the sound *a* as in *pat*, printed in white on the black chart. She indicates a line of *a*'s, single and grouped (*a a aa aaa*) on the wall chart, tells the children what sound the letter represents, and gets them to say it, once or more than once, according to the group she points to. Gradually she speeds up, so that the children get the idea of sounds running into one another. They also practise writing the letter, imitating the arm and hand movements of the teacher. She will then go on to a similar line, of *u*'s as in *up*. Practice is given in pronouncing them singly and in combination with the *as*. The *us* are printed in yellow. When, later on, the *a* of the indefinite article is introduced, it is printed in a deeper yellow to indicate its relationship to *u* and to differentiate it from the *a* of *pat*. This early work is to develop the ability to distinguish shapes, to teach that one must utter a sound as many times as the sign requires, and that the signs may stand for separated or linked sounds according to how they are uttered. Children practise the sounds both orally and by simple exercises in their work books – they may, for instance, supply the middle letter in a word of three letters. When they have attained a certain mastery of sounds the children go on to continuous reading material, and to word-building card games, where the colour is now used to distinguish word classes: e.g. all verbs are on one colour of card. The children make up sentences by arranging the word cards before them.

It is, perhaps, rather surprising that there is no use of colour in the reading material for the scheme other than that already mentioned. The children's first readers are in black and white. The main use of colour is to reinforce the recognition of signs standing for sounds, and for the differentiation of word classes. The scheme can be used without colour, and it might be that the colour is really an irrelevance, except to sugar a phonic approach containing a fair amount of drill. Unfortunately there seems to be little objective evidence on the scheme. Lee (1967) speaks of its success with handicapped children, and refers to an experiment in Ayrshire where 'traditional methods', *Words in Colour*, and the Initial-Teaching Alphabet approach were compared. The results after a year were most in favour of traditional methods; next came *Words in Colour*, and last the Initial Teaching Alphabet. But so few details are given of the design of the experiment – what sort of traditional teaching methods were used, for instance – that we cannot really evaluate the results.

1.2.2 '*Colour Story Reading*' (Jones, 1967)
This scheme also offers aids to pronunciation by the use of

colour. A particular sound in a word is printed on a coloured triangle, circle, or square. Thus a red triangle indicates the pronunciation represented by *a* in the indefinite article, or by *e* in *the*, or by *o* in *lemon*, and will thus back each of these letters. A blue circle indicates a silent letter, and so on. The learner will be helped by colour to differentiate the letter or letter group which resembles another but has a different sound, and that which is different but has the same sound. Contrary to expectations the scheme is not intended to be taught by a phonic method. The teacher has a book, *The Nineteen Stories*, about Mr. Nen and his friends, in which the sounds are used in an amusing fashion. In the first story, for instance, the characters only utter simple vowel sounds. Simple illustrated reading books containing sounds and sentences relevant to each story accompany them.

An experiment, carried out by its author, used each school as its own control. The control group was one year's intake; the experimental group was the next year's intake. Normally the same teacher could take both groups. Publicity and visitors were discouraged. Greater gains in spelling and reading were reported for *Colour Story Reading* than for the more usual black-and-white reading schemes (Jones, 1967). In another experiment Jones, with similar safeguards, compared gains by pupils using the Initial Teaching Alphabet (see below) with those by pupils using *Colour Story Reading*, and found them highly favourable to the latter, in both reading and spelling. Transfer from *Colour Story* to other reading material is of course simple; the coloured shapes are simply left out. Jones felt that the advantage may arise also from the aesthetic appeal of the colours and shapes, and from the high motivating effects of the stories.

1.3 SIMPLIFIED SPELLING

Although, as we have already mentioned, there are various modified spelling systems in existence, they have not always been devised with the problems of learning to read in mind.

Two which we have are the Unifon, in use in the U.S., and the i.t.a., at which we shall look in more detail.

1.3.1   i.t.a

The 'i.t.a.', or Initial Teaching Alphabet, contains forty-four symbols, of which twenty-four are letters from the existing alphabet. It was designed originally by Isaac Pitman in 1837, and revised in recent years by Sir James Pitman.

The Alphabet of i.t.a.[1]

a apple	ɑ father	æ angel	æ author	au bed	b cat	c chair
d doll	ee eel	e egg	f finger	g girl	h hat	ie tie
i ink	j jam	k kitten	l lion	m man	n nest	ŋ king
œ toe	o on	ω book	ꭥ food	ou out	oi oil	p pig
r red	ɼ bird	s soap	ſh ship	ʒ treasure	t tree	th three
th mother	ue due	u up	v van	w window	wh wheel	y yellow
z zoo	ʒ is					

[1] From *An Introduction to the Initial Teaching Alphabet*, i.t.a. Foundation Publication No. 1.

No special shapes are employed for capitals — instead the equivalent small (known as 'lower case') letter is printed in large size. Pitman's hypothesis was that once the child was able to read by i.t.a. he would have no difficulty in transferring his skill to t.o. To this end the i.t.a. letters, especially their upper halves, were kept as similar as possible to t.o., for research has shown that it is chiefly by the upper halves of letters that we recognize them (Huey (1912)). (One can try this out by covering first the upper half, then the lower half of a line of print with a sheet of paper.)

The early history of the i.t.a. movement was unfortunate. It was launched in 1960 in a blaze of publicity, and what was called 'a large scientifically controlled experiment' was begun by the Reading Research Unit of London University Institute of Education in association with the National Foundation for Educational Research. Basically the first experiment compared groups of children learning to read in i.t.a. with groups learning to read in t.o. In an experiment such as this one attempts to choose similar groups of children, otherwise one cannot know whether their progress is due to the reading approach or to something else, such as superior ability. It is not fair to race a hare and a tortoise. These groups of children were matched for such variables as sex, intelligence, and socio-economic status of parents; and for size, location, and type of school, pupil-teacher ratio, and school amenities. The results were a resounding vindication of the claims made for i.t.a. By it children read more quickly and more fluently; and although there was a temporary set-back at transfer in the middle of their second year, by the beginning of the third year the children who had learned i.t.a. first were markedly superior to those who had learned t.o. from the beginning. Reports from the participating schools showed them very enthusiastic (Downing (1964)). Unfortunately this first experiment was suspect in design. For one thing, there was no attempt to see that the teachers were equally skilled – yet research indicates that the teacher is one of the most important factors in learning to read. For another, the reading time was not equated between the two groups; yet it is fairly obvious that a class that spends, say, twice as much time on reading as another class will progress better, whatever reading scheme is used. Again, the matched classes were in different schools, which might account for differences in achievement. There was, too, the 'Hawthorne effect' – the gain which it seems likely experimental groups make merely from the fact that they are using new materials and are the centre of interest. Stott (1964) and Southgate (1965) make some severe criticisms of the experiment – the i.t.a. children had a national spotlight focused upon them, they had new books, the teachers were given special attention – that are not completely answered by the experiments (Downing and Jones (1966)). They report a second experiment, which meets some of the objections. There was little publicity, the parallel classes were in the same schools, and were taught by the same teacher in i.t.a. and t.o. The i.t.a. results were still superior, but less so than in the first experiment. Despite precautions to the contrary, it appears that the teachers did spend more time with their i.t.a. groups, and this may have affected the results.

As time goes on and the original publicity and enthusiasm fade, so that more objective experiments become possible, a more detached evaluation of i.t.a. may be made. In 1969 *i.t.a.: an Independent Evaluation*, by F. W. Warburton and Vera Southgate, was published. This was a study commissioned by the Schools Council. They did two things: (i) evaluated seventeen pieces of research on i.t.a.; (ii) collected and appraised the views of knowledgeable people (teachers, advisers, lecturers) closely connected with the use of i.t.a. Of the pieces of research all but six were found suspect in design, or to be comparing whole teaching schemes rather than simply the t.o. and i.t.a. alphabets. Six only provided the same reading material in both alphabets and were thus considered satisfactory in this important respect. (They are not completely satisfactory, however; different media and different methods require different reading material for their most efficient functioning.) As a way of learning to read these researchers showed i.t.a. to be superior to look-and-say approaches employing t.o.; they offered no evidence about the merits of phonic schemes in t.o. Again, in the other part of the investigation, knowledgeable people were found to be in favour of t.o. as against whatever traditional approach they had been acquainted with. (There is, however, a difficulty in asking people committed to a course of action whether they have made the right choice: we often do not admit, even to ourselves, that we have made an error.)

What are we in a position to say about i.t.a., bearing in mind the Report and other studies?

(1) Evidence accumulates that it enables children to learn to read more quickly, but there is nothing to show that at the age of eight these children have any advantage over those who learnt in t.o. (See Warburton and Southgate (1969), p. 275; Cartwright and Jones (1967), p. 71.)

(2) There is no evidence that it is the 'best' learning-to-read medium. All we know is that, according to the Report, it can have advantages over some teaching by look-and-say. (However, of the seventeen researches discussed in that Report, several that were unsatisfactory in design did not favour i.t.a. There is no reason to suppose that had their design been different they would necessarily have favoured i.t.a.) Again, the i.t.a. alphabet is unsatisfactory in various ways (see, e.g., Stott); yet some publishers have made heavy investments in i.t.a. type. There are pieces of research not emphasized in the Warburton report which seem to show that other media, such as that in *Colour Story Reading*, may be better (see 1.2.2 above).

(3) All the evidence we have on reading suggests that there are other factors more important in learning to read than the particular means employed; and that means which work with one child, or for one teacher, won't work so well with another child and for another teacher. The Report found schools with t.o. teaching doing every bit as well as i.t.a. schools.

All we can say about i.t.a. at the moment, therefore, is that it takes its place as one acceptable medium in which to learn to read.

1.4 TRADITIONAL ORTHOGRAPHY

It is, naturally, quite impossible to describe all the t.o. reading schemes which have been devised — the overwhelming majority. Standard schemes at the moment tend to be basically look-and-say — the *Janet and John Readers* (Nisbet) in the U.K., for instance. What we shall do, therefore, is to say a little about several schemes which are notable or unusual in some way.

2. *SCHEMES*

The first two described are phonic approaches. It is often said, and there is a certain amount of research evidence for it, that phonic methods are not suited to less able readers. However, the authors of these two schemes dispute this.

2.1   *The Programmed Reading Kit* (D. H. Stott, 1962) Stott's work with ten subnormal teenagers led him to develop a phonic approach. These boys were completely unable to read. Attempts to get them to build up a minimum sight vocabulary by look-and-say methods had failed. Stott devised a series of games through which the learner acquired step by step the ability to recognize, analyse, and synthesize sounds. Thus the first game was with 'Morris-cards', cards with a picture of an object on one side, and the initial letter of that object on the other. The learner had several cards in front of him and had to recognize the letter when the teacher named the object: if she said 'bed', he would be expected to pick up the 'b' card, and so on.

The kit aims to build up phonic skills and is used without reading books at first, the motivation being provided by success in the games, and not by the ability to understand printed matter. It was intended for backward adolescents, but has been used with modifications for infants (Stott (1964)).

2.2   *The Royal Road Readers* (Daniels and Diack, 1954) Daniels and Diack conducted research (reported later, 1956, 1958) on which their *Royal Road Readers* scheme is based. In their Teacher's Book to the series they discuss the limitations of traditional methods and recommend a revised phonic method. In contrast with methods which limit vocabulary, theirs limits phonic complexity, giving as large a vocabulary as is within the child's comprehension. Thus in their first reader they use only words in which no letter is silent, and in which each letter has its most common sound value: 'The letters *g* and *c* are always hard as in *pig* and *cat*, and the vowels short as in *cat*, *leg*, *pin*, *hot* and *rug*.' However, they consider interest as important, and add to such words about forty others which do not fulfil these conditions. Later books add progressively to the phonics.

The basis of a look-and-say method lies in its requirement of *general* distinctions between the shapes of words. This phonic method, however, concentrates on the exact distinctions brought about by individual letters. Thus instead of varying the lengths of words as some sight, and some phonic, methods do, the authors begin with words of the same length *hat*, *bat*, *man*, *nib*, etc.; an early exercise requires the learner to supply the missing letter in words as similar as *bed*, *red*, *leg*, *fox*, *net*. In its concentration on words *and* sounds, rather than on sounds, this method differs from many phonic methods, and is called the 'phonic word method'. It differs from others also in the emphasis the authors place on meaning; before the end of Book I the first story is introduced, which is a 'milestone in the reading experiences of the child'. Because of his training so far it is real 'unseen' reading, 'not the parroting of over-familiar sentences'.

Most reading schemes make a direct approach by one method or another to reading. The one described next, however, lays less emphasis on the single skill of reading and more on its place in the development of the communication skills generally.

2.3   The 'Language Experience' Approach

'Language experience' under that title is an American approach associated with the name of Roach Van Allen.

It assumes that the child whose language ability is developed will find learning to read a simple, almost incidental matter. Thus it attempts to provide a rich background of experiences from which the child draws things to listen to, and to talk, read, or write about, and no distinction is made between the development of reading skills and that of listening, speaking, and writing skills. 'Rather than attempting to judge each child's progress in terms of specific language skills, the teacher should determine whether the whole programme reveals a developing pattern of language experiences, with each child learning from repeated work that: *what he thinks about he can say*; *what he says can be written and dictated*; *what has been written can be read* (Allen and Allen, (1967), p. 1).

It is difficult to describe the approach in detail, because of the wide variety of experiences it provides and techniques it advocates. It has two aspects. One is called the 'continuing language programme', the aim of which is to provide a wealth of visual and auditory stimuli through books, films, and film-strips; records of music, song, poetry, sounds, and dances; and many opportunities for self-expression by means of the ready availability of all kinds of writing, drawing, painting, and modelling materials. The other aspect is represented by the 'pupil book', which is topic based and contains extracts, questions, suggestions for activities, and opportunities for responses, many of them open-ended.

In the initial stages one characteristic procedure is for the child to respond to something that interests him, perhaps a pet, by talk and by drawing it. The teacher will write down the naming word for it, say *dog*, which the child will trace or copy. She will then require a sentence or 'story' about it from the child himself: it might be *My dog barks*, which the child will write and read, and illustrate. Several of his 'stories' may be stapled into a reading book. The book produced by the child himself will form part of the corpus of reading matter for himself and for his group. Thus the vocabulary of his stories is controlled by his own oral language. The books he has produced will form part of the stock of the reading 'corner', supplemented by various sorts of printed matter – books of several levels, magazines, newspapers, reference books. There is also a 'writing corner' containing charts of letters, to help with letter formation; elementary dictionaries; the beginnings of word lists, to which children can add (e.g. rhyming words, words with similar sounds, words with related meanings); an ideas file, containing cards with ten words on particular topics for a story or poem; a file of 'story starters' (first few lines); and a 'things to do' file to invite writing activities.

The technique for reading acquisition in this approach is essentially a sentence method. *The Harvard Report on Reading in Elementary Schools* (Austin and Morrison, 1963) thinks the language-experience approach has dangers. If the teacher fails to correct errors in the pupil's language or spelling in order not to discourage his creativity, questionable habits may be formed, especially since his writing is used for reading matter. And again, memorization rather than reading may be the more likely result with material he has produced himself. On the other hand, the Report is in agreement with claims made for the approach – that it is likely to produce high interest and motivation; a sense of the inter-relatedness of communication processes, and of the importance of reading as one of them; and that it fosters creative expression.

3. *LINGUISTICS AND READING*

We shall look now at approaches to reading from a linguistics standpoint.

3.1 *Linguistics and the Teaching of Reading* (Carl A. Lefevre, 1964)

Lefevre's book has a title similar to that of Fries (see 3.3 below), but the diagnosis of the problems and the solution he suggests are very different. Fries is concerned with 'spelling-pattern' contrasts between individual words. Lefevre, however, considers that a concern with individual words rather than with words in context has been responsible for 'word calling', where a learner can sound single words in a sentence but they do not 'add up' for him to a meaningful statement:

To comprehend printed matter, the reader must perceive entire language structures as wholes – as unitary meaning bearing patterns. Short of this level of perception the reader simply does not perceive those total language structures that alone are capable of carrying meaning. He may perceive individual words as if words were meaning-bearing units in themselves, one of the most serious of all disabilities. Or he may group words visually in structureless pattern fragments that do not and cannot bear meaning (Ch. XI).

There is exaggeration here: individual words can be 'meaning-bearing' units: *cat* is clearly meaningful. If we find a word in isolation we give it its most common meaning. Nevertheless, what Lefevre says is true; meaning inheres in patterns rather than in individual words. Thus in 'He was given the cat by the bosun' we have no reason to suspect that 'given' and 'cat' are used in anything but their most common sense until the sentence is complete, when we realize that the man may have been flogged, though we still cannot be sure until even more of the context has been revealed to us. Were the sentence 'He was given the cat by the vicar' we could be surer that the most probable meanings apply (but not absolutely sure without further context – there have been sadistic vicars). Thus Lefevre insists that in English the individual word is an unstable element, 'whether it is taken as a semantic or as a structural unit; that is to say whether, for instance, 'cat' represents *animal* or *whip* in the sentence quoted (semantic), or whether 'strike' is a noun or a verb, as in 'the strike is over' or 'the men will strike' (structural).

Lefevre's is a sentence approach, since he argues that in native-language learning the speaker develops linguistic control by working in from larger structural patterns to smaller (p. 31). Pre-reading experience is, of course, essential: 'Probably the best way to prepare a very young child for reading is to hold him in your lap and read aloud to him, over and over again, stories which he likes from the world's treasury of literature, *while the child follows the text with eyes and ears.* Thus with the printed page before him, the learner enjoys a real introduction to the relationship of graphic symbols to language. The printed page talks' (p. 36). Reading readiness has arrived when he realizes that speech may be written and print may be spoken, for he already possesses the basic signals and structures in his speech – he has merely to develop consciousness of them in relation to the graphic system. For speaking intonation the writer advises: 'Probably the best method is *practice in speaking and oral reading of familiar patterns, with emphasis on the native intonations*' (p. 43). And speaking of language patterns, he says 'The best method would be to teach the child to read and write the language patterns he brings to school with him. . . . *Let him first learn to read and write his own patterns*, 'corrected' only insofar as necessary to bring them in line with the common patterns of sentence functions and word order as they have been described by linguists' (p. 80).

Lefevre's approach is appropriately tentative and he does not go into detail over classroom procedure. On occasions when he does approach the classroom, he sometimes causes the reader some anxiety about what he actually intends: 'In school [the child] should become conscious of abstract sentence patterns, and learn to use simple formulas for them' (p. 83), and this anxiety is not quite dispelled by his assurance that children take to these as games in the hands of the right teacher. In general, however, his other suggestions show a fine awareness of classroom actualities and the needs and interests of young children.

3.2 *Breakthrough to Literacy* (MacKay, Thompson and Schaub, 1970)

The approach has many similarities to that of both Van Allen and Lefevre described above. It offers a 'theory of literacy' which resembles that of the 'language-experience' approach – that children should read *and* write from the beginning of their literary training. The authors claim 'The emphasis we came to place on *production* in the first stages of learning to read is one of the places where we depart from the basic assumptions of traditional teaching methods in this field.' A basic piece of apparatus in this scheme is a folder of cards with simple familiar words printed on them, similar in principle to those used by Gattegno (1962) and others. The child composes his own sentences by choosing and arranging the cards. There is a similar folder of cards with letters on them to help the child spell words. Thus from the first the child is producing as well as reading his own language. There are also graded reading books appealing to the children's interests. Great stress is laid on the conventional readers are narrowly and out-datedly middle-class and have little appeal for the majority. The scheme is based on sound principles, and it is a pity the title, *Breakthrough to Literacy*, overclaims on their originality.

3.3   *Linguistics and Reading* (Charles C. Fries, 1962)

Fries neatly describes the process of learning to read in his Chapter IV. He quotes authorities who have described tech-niques necessary for reading that involves understanding, thinking, imagining, judging, evaluating, analysing, reason-ing, and so on; but comments that these must be developed through the uses of language: they do not constitute the read-ing process. He goes on:

The process of learning to read in one's native language is the *process of transfer* from the auditory signs for language signals, which the child has already learned, to the new visual signs for the same signals. This process of transfer is not the learning of the language code or of a new language code; it is not the learning of a new or different set of language signals. It is not the learning of new 'words'; or of new grammatical structures, or of new meanings (p. 120).

Learning to read, therefore, means developing a *consider-able range of habitual responses* to a specific set of patterns of graphic shapes. Habits develop only out of practice. The *teaching* of beginning reading, to children of four or five, must be conceived not in terms of the imparting of knowledge but in terms of opportunities for practice. Fries speaks of three stages of learning to read. The first is the transfer stage. The second is when response to immediate signals becomes automatic, and the reader can supply responses to those portions of them which are not in the graphic representations themselves – tone sequences, stresses, pauses, and so on; here he relies on his cumulative comprehension of meaning. The third stage is when it is used equally with the spoken language in the acquiring and developing of experience.

Fries suggests that stage one should be achieved by what he calls the 'spelling-pattern' approach, which he distinguishes from a phonics approach. Much phonics teaching assumes that the process consists in learning to match words as written, letter by letter, with words as pronounced, sound by sound. But if we take MAN/MANE/MEAN the single letter A does not indicate the vowel sound, but the whole spelling pattern of any one in contrast to the others. Because Fries does not want confusion from any single sound of a letter, his first step is to teach the names of the letters and the recognition of their shapes. The next stage is to teach progressive recognition of spelling patterns and contrasts, the procedure being that the teacher pronounces *in normal talking fashion* each new word and each pair of contrastive words as it is introduced, and makes sure that the pupil, from the pronunciation, identifies the words as ones he knows. One group of spelling patterns would be A CAT BATS AT A RAT

Fries does not put his ideas into a specific reading scheme, though he originally devised the approach to teach his son to read. On the face of it, it seems that the motivation of the pupils would be low with such abstract material. But Fries quite specifically excludes attempts at contextualization: 'Seeking an extraneous interest in a story as a story, during the earliest steps of the transfer stage is more likely to hinder than to help the efforts put forth by the pupil himself' (p. 199). This statement would not command general agreement, and Fries's approach is in marked contrast to some others also claiming a linguistic standpoint, notably that of Lefevre.

4. THE PLACE OF METHOD, MEDIA, AND SCHEMES

Wherever large-scale research has been carried out no single method, medium, or scheme of learning to read has proved better than any other (see for example the UNESCO survey conducted by Gray (1956); and the review of research by Russell and Fea (1963)). The work of Morris (1966) and Ramsey (1962) spoken of in Chapter VIII, 1.4 above suggests that other factors are far more important. Morris, in her impressive survey in Kent, finds that the quality of the principal and that of staff, in that order, override other factors. Southgate emphasizes the total situation, the most important variable being 'the attitude towards reading which is prevalent in the school and the consequent reading drive in force' (Warburton and Southgate (1969), p. 175).

It is, however, no use saying we require good teachers and attitudes, and considering all problems solved when, if ever, we have them. Even good teachers are by no means always successful. We have seen that many other factors operate. This is recognized when we talk of 'reading readiness'. Thus Russell (1961) gives a check-list for reading readiness which has as main headings Physical, Social, Emotional and Psychological Readiness. Such lists have their dangers if they encourage us to delay reading until all the signs have appeared; but they are useful in reminding us that learning to read is one aspect of a general growth of the personality.

But learning to read is also, and centrally, a matter of *language*. Unless he has some language already, the child cannot read language. All the other variables in the situation, important though they may be, must be subordinate to this. Work in the past has often done less than justice to this fact. Certainly 'reading-readiness tests', for example, contain linguistic items – vocabulary, word matching, remembering the sequence of words in a story. But such tests tend to concentrate on vocabulary rather than syntax; they do not look at the child's knowledge of language, his awareness of the possibilities of language, in the sense we have attempted to define it in this book. It would seem that a systematic study of the relationship between reading and pre-reading oracy is one of the most important of our tasks over the next few years.

5. SUMMARY

We have been concerned with three main means of simplifying the *medium* or 'signalling system' of words spelt in the conventional alphabet – by marking similar sounds, by printing them in colour, and by using a more logical alphabet. Various general approaches or schemes attempt to help the new reader in the traditional alphabet. Some of these have a linguistics standpoint. However, learning to read is not primarily a matter of learning to read – i.e. of the method, medium or scheme employed. It is rather a matter of the general development of the pupil, and, it is suggested, particularly of his linguistic development.

CHAPTER X

ORACY AND READING

1. *READING SKILLS*

In Chapter VI we looked at the processes involved in language reception. We said that it was convenient to think of these under four headings:

1. Recognition.
2. Use of constraints.
3. Organization.
4. Understanding.

We were then thinking particularly about the reception of the *spoken* language, but what we said then applies, with one or two provisos, to the written language also, to reading. In recognition we are concerned with visual symbols — words made up of letters — rather than with sound symbols. When we use constraints we have much less help from phonological constraints; but we are given literal constraints, help from letter sequences, which we also looked at in Chapter VI. Otherwise the basic processes are the same. We may thus refer the reader back to the discussion of these matters and concern ourselves here with the one element not so far considered — recognition in reading.

1.2   RECOGNITION

Let us try to distinguish the various means by which we recognize words. First we may make a distinction between identifying them and understanding them. We might 'identify' the word *xxzpq*, in the sense that we distinguish it from other words like *lapislazuli*, without understanding it. In this process of identification we use various means:

(i) *Letter identification*

These three letters make up a word: ▯□▯ . We know this is not the word □□□ because the letter shapes are different. Letter-shape is one of the things which helps us to differentiate one word from another. Letters at the beginning or end of a word, double letters like *oo*, unusual letters (*k, x, qu*) seem to be particularly helpful.

(ii) *Word-shape identification*

We also know that the word ▯□▯ is different from □□□, because the shape of one word is ⌐┘ and of the other ⌐┐ .

(iii) *Letter order*

We also know that ▯□▯ is not the same as ▯▯□ . This seems obvious. Suppose, however, the shapes stood for people, a tall one, a medium-sized one, and a small one; if we saw them together today, and we saw them together tomorrow, we might say we saw the same three people. A child similarly could consider them the 'same' unless he knew that order is important. Thus he might confuse 'hat' and 'the', or, when he came to write, spell 'the' as 'hte' or 'teh').

(iv) *Letter position*

We also know that ▯ is not the same as □□□ . This requires learning by the child. After all, in the world of objects he is accustomed to it and it does not matter whether the book is *standing* on a shelf, or *lying* on a table, it is still the same object; a cup with handle to left or right is still a cup, whereas *b* differs from *d*.

So far, then, we have been identifying letters and words by shape and order alone, using neither sound nor meaning. Which clues are used will depend on the word in question and on the approach of the reader. It seems clear, however, that the emphasis which advocates of look-and-say placed on the whole word, claiming support from *Gestalt* psychology (see Ch. VII, 2.1 above), was excessive. There are several reasons for this; our capacity to distinguish shapes as shapes is limited – if there are many of them we get confused; in any case, many children beginning to read appear to perceive not the whole word but the individual letters. Rickard (1935) has shown that although many short common words are of the same shape children have little difficulty in recognizing them, thus demonstrating that they must be using other clues. None of this means that children cannot acquire vocabulary by look-and-say methods: they obviously do, making use, however, of two or more of several possible visual clues. In other words, the practice of the method is wiser than some of the theories used to support it.

Hitherto we have identified words and letters by shape alone – the symbols used above have neither sound nor meaning, and yet we can recognize them. But the words in the English language started as sounds before ever they were written down. When we are learning to read we revive these sounds and their associated meanings.

(v) *Sound identification – letter*

Letters usually represent sounds, though not always the same sounds. It depends on such factors as their arrangement and position (and of course there are 'silent' letters). Suppose ☐ represents the *p* sound in *porridge*, ☐ represents the *o* sound in *orange*, and ☐ the *g* sound in *pig*. From the letters ☐☐☐ we get the sounds *p – o – g* and build up the sound *pog*.

(vi) *Sound identification – group*

After the initial stages of reading there is no need to sound individual letters. We become familiar with the sound whole groups make. We may suppose that the letter combination ☐☐ is common, as is *sch* or *all* or *ing*, in our alphabet. We find that on seeing ☐☐ the sound we may represent as *pog* comes instantly to us.

(vii) *Sound identification – words*

Similarly we become familiar with the sounds complete words make. The word *rapple* can be pronounced instantly by anybody reading this book for the first time, though he can never have seen it before, since it is invented. It is important to note that the child needs to learn that the symbols for letters, groups, and words on the page stand for sounds, in the order in which they appear. (There are rare exceptions to this – the Scottish pronunciation of *what – hwat –* for instance.)

Thus in reading there are visual clues and there are phonic clues to enable us to identify a word. We may not, however, know its meaning. The case has similarities with that of people who learnt a foreign language at school, and can, if pushed, read it aloud with something like the right pronunciation, but who no longer understand what they are reading.

The usual condition of our understanding the meaning of a word is that we have met it before, and know what it refers to, its 'referent'. The child who, by sight and sound clues, understands 'elephant' does so because the word is already in his mind as referring to that large cynical beast he saw last week at the zoo, and the word in his mind and the word on the page suddenly coincide.

Of course there are other words which have no external referents – we have called them 'structure words'. But they are already present in the reader's mind. This coincidence, this coming together, of the word on the page and the word already in the mind, is the realization of meaning. Some phrases are so common that we may do the same with them: *How do you do, Good morning, Once upon a time,* for instance.

Can we sum up so far? Learning to recognize words in reading is like playing a slightly different game of snap. When the word in our mind corresponds with the word on the page, we as it were cry 'snap' – the word acquires significance for us.

These skills of recognition are sometimes referred to as the 'Primary Reading Skills': for the next order of skills, the use of constraints, Merritt (1969) in a valuable paper has suggested the term 'Intermediate Skills' to distinguish them from the Higher-Order Reading Skills involving ability to understand and evaluate a variety of reading materials. It is beyond the scope of this book to pursue these; as Fries points out (4 below) in another connection, they may be rather language and thinking skills, possessed by someone unable to read. We shall, however, look at Intermediate Skills in the next section.

2. THE PROCESS OF READING

Clearly the primary reading skill must be that of recognition, in the sense that unless the learner can recognize a word he cannot predict what comes next, or for that matter what went before. However, it is easy to exaggerate the importance of this, in that immediately even a very few words are recognized the child can bring to bear the ability to use contextual constraints which he has developed in the spoken language. But we will defer the discussion of this to the next section, and examine the use the mature reader makes of such constraints.

We take a sentence chosen more or less at random (from the *Harvard Report on Reading*, Austin & Morrison, 1963, p. 7):

Over the past few decades/the classroom teacher/, more than any other/, has suffered slings and arrows from outraged educators,/would-be educators/, and so-called educators/when surveys of reading instruction/have revealed serious shortcomings/

Let us consider how a skilled reader reads this. He recognizes the words, and groups them according to his expectations (syntactic, semantic, phonological). Thus they will probably be grouped in some such way as we have marked. We do not really know whether he can take in a whole phrase like 'Over the past few decades' all at once, or whether he takes in the words successively and with immense rapidity.* When he has

* The eye does not travel continuously along a line of print, but stops several times, and it is in these pauses that the reading is done. The pauses are called 'fixations'. Anderson & Dearborn (1952) demonstrate that the skilled reader's eye has six or seven fixations in reading a line (stops six or seven times), and takes in up to five words per fixation.

read the first phrase, he probably does not remember the exact words, but stores the message, and goes on to the next with certain expectations aroused: *syntactically* a nominal group acting as subject is probable, not a verbal group (e.g., just such a phrase as 'the classroom teacher, not such as' have revealed serious shortcomings'); *semantically* (because the book is on reading) a phrase such as 'Egyptian belly dancer' is improbable; *phonologically* the pitch is held up at 'decades' in anticipation of the subject. (But the reader is also glancing ahead, and so may mentally stress *classroom* teacher, in contrast to what will follow.) Had the phrase 'Egyptian belly dancer' occurred, the reader would still be able to recognize it from a variety of clues, though his semantic prediction had been frustrated – but he would be puzzled, and grow increasingly puzzled as the sentence progressed.

Over the past few decades/the Egyptian belly dancer/more than any other/has suffered the slings and arrows . . .

The sentence would not really 'make sense' for him. (We shall return to the belly dancer in a moment.) In turn 'the classroom teacher' raises expectations of all three kinds about what will follow; and so on. A child in the early stages of reading might take in a single word at a time. Even so, these words would raise expectations which would help him to recognize what follows.

This would be more difficult for him if he had learned to read words exclusively from lists. In that case he would give the word the connotation it most commonly had for him. Take the word 'over', with which the passage starts. This might easily signify for him 'above' ('the plane was over the house'), or 'finished' ('school was over'), or, if he played cricket in the garden, 'six balls in succession'. In none of these senses could he understand the use of 'over' in 'he was over the river' or 'the foreman was over the workmen' or 'a few presents left over'. Nor could he understand 'over' as used in the sentence referred to. One has only to glance at the *Oxford English Dictionary* to be surprised at the numerous generally-used meanings many common words have: these the educated adult employs accurately and automatically from his linguistic experience, but the young learner is not in the same advantageous position. The adult has knowledge of the occurrence of particular words in a large variety of contexts, mostly spoken contexts. The young child has a limited amount of such knowledge. If he is of average ability he will be acquainted with many common words in context. His reading could, however, be interfered with if he had met 'over' in a list, thought of it as meaning 'above' ('higher than'), and found it in his reading book as 'school is over now'. What, he might think, is it over?

The relevance of this to our general discussion at this point is that, as we have seen in Chapter VI, prediction implies a knowledge of the possible usages of words, the possible choices one may make. Take 'Over the past few decades'. Before the word 'over' is selected there is an immense variety of choices open. The occurrence of 'the' establishes for us that a prepositional use has been chosen, and the two words, together with semantic constraints, determine that 'past' must be adjectival. Had the sentence, however, begun 'In the past few decades . . .' we should have reached 'few' before being certain that 'past' was not a noun. This would have involved also phonological prediction that there was no pause between 'past' and 'few'. After all, the sentence might have read 'In the past, few decades were more noted for their success in teaching reading . . .'

The reader will by now be anxious to return to the Egyptian belly dancer whom we left a few paragraphs ago. Substituted for 'the classroom teacher' in the paragraph we quoted she would cause some confusion in any one perusing the book, not because the words are hard to recognize, or because syntactic or phonological constraints are thwarted, but because semantic expectations are frustrated. Let us forget for the moment that the sentence is from a book on reading. Let us imagine we meet it in isolation. Shall we still feel confused? For a good part of the passage we shall not. After all, a 'belly dancer' might well suffer 'slings and arrows' from 'outraged educators'; and the phrase 'revealed serious shortcomings' might easily occur in connection with her. It is the phrase 'when surveys of reading instruction' that puts the dancer out of context, and then, when we know this, some of the others push in that direction as well. Syntactic and phonological constraints show themselves in the words preceding the word or phrase in question. Semantic constraints do this certainly. But they may also occur afterwards, as this example demonstrates. Although our understanding of a sentence grows as we read further into it, we may be in a position of having to revise our estimate of its meaning several times before the end. Semantic constraints lie also in the surrounding text – i.e, in this case, the fact that we have a book about reading before us. Knowing this we could conclude with a fair degree of certainty that 'Egyptian belly dancer' was the result of some aberration on the part of author or type-setter.

3. USE OF CONSTRAINTS BY THE YOUNG CHILD

We have seen in Chapter VI. 4 that young children make use of constraints in the oral language. It is what we have called their knowledge of the possibilities of language. It now remains for us to show this process at work when they come to read.

Here is an extract from a recording of a conversation with a boy of four years six months. He cannot read at all, but is following the story the adult is reading to him. The boy makes use of the constraints in the language, pictures, and total situation, to contribute to the reading:

Let's try this one. A little yellow bird flew high in the . . .
sky
Looking for a place to build . . .
a nest
Can I build my nest in your . . .
basket

He asked the black...
puppy
No room said...
the puppy
Where shall I build my...
nest
Asked the...
bird
It would not be safe here on the...
ground
She flew over a farm. Shall I build my...
nest
Under the green roof or in the red chimney?
No. He couldn't could he?
No. The farmer's wife wore a red scarf round her...
neck
It's not safe to build here she...
said
There are too many...
things about
What sort of things?
Don't know

'A little yellow bird flew high in the – *sky*' is a semantic and collocational prediction. The word was actually *air* – but of course the boy had no sight recognition. 'Build – *a nest*', 'On – *the ground*', 'Scarf round her – *neck*', 'There are too many – *things about*' are the same. Verbs are predicted as well as nouns: 'It's not safe to build, she – *said*'. And inversion is understood: 'Asked the – *bird*'. The fact that some of the predictions are incorrect in terms of the text is unimportant: obviously the boy only needs to be able to decipher minimal visual prompts (e.g. *h* not *n* for *head* not *neck*, for instance) and he will be reading.

Skill in using constraints is based on an awareness of the possible choices which might be made. Here the boy is experimenting:

He thought he saw a fish wave back with its . . .
hand
No
paw
Yes

The word was in fact *fin*: but the boy moves from the most probable, in his terms (to wave with the *hand*), to a prediction which takes into account that the situation requires a non-human word, and this for the time being, the adult accepts.

We may say, therefore, that the use of constraints is very important in learning to read. But this is only one aspect of a general linguistic ability which we may hope for in children. We have characterized this ability as *an awareness of the possibilities of language.*

4. *READING AND TRANSFER*

We have spoken about recognition as the basic reading skill. If we recognize a word we must have met it before. We meet most of our words for the first time through our ears, as part of the spoken language, though we meet some for the first time in books. There is no doubt, however, that the child approaching reading must have become familiar with his total vocabulary in spoken form.

When he comes to read, therefore, he is not faced with the problem of learning a new language such as the native tongue he acquired a year or two before. What he has to do is in a sense far simpler – to recognize a different symbol, a sight not a sound symbol, for the same thing. We have already looked at Fries's account of the process (Ch. IX, 3.3). He writes, it will be remembered: 'The process of learning to read in one's native language is *the process of transfer* from the auditory signs for language symbols, which the child has already learned, to the new visual signs for the same signals' (p. 120). He emphasizes that other skills sometimes thought of as an essential part of the reading process are really a matter of *general* linguistic development: '... we certainly confuse the issue if we insist that (the) use of reading and stimulating and cultivating the techniques of thinking, evaluating, and so on, *constitutes the reading process*.' Such thinking abilities, he points out, may be developed and have been achieved by people who could not read.

Reading, then, is a process of transfer. We have, as it were, to recognize (on British Railways, for instance) that the *sound* of a whistle has a visual alternative — the waving of a green flag: by both of these the train guard may say to the engine driver 'Proceed'. There are naturally differences between the written and spoken languages, both in their form and in how they were used; and this is one of the reasons for letting children read their own spoken language in some reading schemes. Again, in the spoken language children learnt words as wholes, whereas in the written language, by the phonic method, they have to build them up. But it is easy to overestimate such differences; what needs emphasizing is that many children come to reading equipped with a powerful array of relevant reading skills, which enable them to learn to read in an apparently effortless way.

5. *SPOKEN AND WRITTEN LANGUAGE IN READING*

One of the main aims of a project already referred to (Strickland (1962)) was to investigate the relationship of the language of text books used in the teaching of reading to the language of elementary school children. Samples were analysed of each reading book of the six grade levels of four widely used U.S. reading series. On this basis the findings were that patterns of sentence structure were introduced rather haphazardly, and often not followed up by any sort of repetition or effort at mastery, there being no over-all scheme for grading structures as there was for vocabulary. However, the general conclusion was that 'The oral language children use is far more advanced than the language of books in which they are taught to read'

(p. 106). In view of this, and the further finding of the report that 'children learn fairly thoroughly at an early age the basic structures of their language' (p. 106), it would seem that there is little point in a strict grading of patterns. Strickland then raises the question as to 'whether children would be aided or hindered by the use of sentences in their books more like the sentences they use in speech'.

This is an interesting point. Certain reading schemes make it a central concern that the children should learn to read the sentences they themselves have produced, even before they are at a stage to write them down. Van Allen's remark may be remembered: 'What [the child] thinks about he can say and what he says can be written and dictated; what has been written can be read' (see Ch. IX, 2.3); and MacKay, Thompson, and Schaub (1970) base their scheme on word cards, so that the child makes sentences before he can write (see Ch. IX, 3.2). Examples of children's sentences produced under this last scheme range from:

I am happy. I am big. I am a big girl. Are you?

to:

Concorde can fly. My mum went to the hairdresser's last night and my dad said she looked beautiful. My dad kissed my mum. Princess Anne launched the *Esso Northumbria* (p. 20).

It is at once clear from these sentences that their value lies in the fact that they are interesting to the children who produce them, and not that they are particularly *spoken* sentences. Those beginning *My mum*, and *My Dad* certainly are: but *Princess Anne launched the Esso Northumbria* is not particularly so, and the first group are obviously not; any child would elide the *I am* to *I'm*. In other words, the distinction we have to draw is rather between interesting and dull material than between spoken and written. We could not, after all, have a book in completely spoken language; it would be very hard to read, and open to misunderstanding. It might be that some popular reading books are too middle-class for many children (who in England refer to *my mum* instead of *mummy* or *mother*), but this is a feature of their intrinsic interest for such children. One of the functions of written material as distinct from spoken is to contain well-formed sentences, and it seems that these will make for easier assimilation in the earlier stages of reading by their regularity, and thus their easier predictability. In Chapter III we spoke of how adults intuitively use well-formed sentences when talking to young children, and there is some parallel here. One more point needs to be made. It is common to poke fun at the artificiality of some readers containing sentences like 'Can Dad fan Nan'. These are phonic readers; their approach is different, but they have much formidable theory and much effective practice behind them. Teaching children to read their own speech will not teach them to build up new words phonically.

In fact, there is a good deal of confusion in discussions of this topic about what is meant by spoken and written sentences. It will be quite clear to the reader in Chapter II, 3 of this book that *some* spoken English would be quite unreadable. A piece of research commonly quoted is that by Ruddell (1965), which concludes:

1. Reading comprehension is a function of the similarity of patterns of language structure in the reading material to oral patterns of language structure used by children.

2. Reading comprehension scores on materials that utilize high frequency patterns of oral language structure are significantly greater than reading comprehension scores on materials that utilize low frequency patterns of oral language structure.

There is only one example given of each type: a high-frequency pattern of oral language structure (i.e. one occurring commonly) is like *A spaceman/could fix/the small hole;* a low-frequency pattern is like *The leader/gave/the men/short breaks/because they needed a rest*. If we may judge from these examples, there is nothing particularly oral about them; no doubt the first type occurs in the spoken language more often than the second, but the probability is that it does so in the written language also. After all, the first pattern is subject-verb-object, one of the basic patterns of the grammatical system. All the research seems to be saying is that children find material written in simple patterns easier to understand than that written in more complex patterns. But then nobody would recommend that they should start on Johnsonian sentences.

We may sum up by saying that the language children read, whether their own, or that in reading books, should be interesting to them, using words that they understand, most of which will be from the spoken language. But most of the sentences they meet should be well-formed, and thus probably nearer to the written language than to the spoken as the tape-recorder hears it.

6. READING AND PRIOR KNOWLEDGE

Learning to read is a matter of drawing on one's prior knowledge. Children normally have a larger vocabulary and knowledge of structures than they will encounter in their reading books. They have some knowledge of life, and thus they have valid expectations about what will be said in their reading books: mouths *talk*, they do not *walk*; trees *grow*, they do not *row*; and so on. Now certainly one of the functions of reading will be to develop in the reader new and unusual ideas; imaginative stories, for instance, may have trees *talk-ing* and *walking*, and metaphorical language works on a similar combination of the unexpected elements. But these usages are often modifications of familiar semantic ones already deeply established in the learner, and the mature reader is within his experience of language and usage. In all these ways reading is a matter of using the skill and knowledge one already has. It is not *just* transfer, of course – one has never spoken the sentences one meets in books; but on the whole one will have met all the elements – vocabulary and structure – which one has to organize. But then this organization and understanding is, as we have seen, a general linguistic and thinking process, not specifically a reading process.

Linguists such as Bloomfield (Bloomfield and Barnhard (1961)), Hall (1964) and Fries (1963) felt it so important to isolate what they considered to be the primary reading skill – an ability to translate visual symbols into sounds – that they tend to play down meaning. Thus Hall (1964) writes: 'The ultimate test of any method of teaching reading is whether the learner can deal with nonsense syllables; if a child cannot read off *glump*, *trip*, or *dank*, not caring whether these syllables have a real life meaning or not, the method has failed' (p.432). Bloomfield was so indifferent to the context, both linguistic and non-linguistic (context of situation), that he would reject pictures in reading books as being distracting and irrelevant. Fries, as we have already seen (Ch. IX, 3.3), would object to the pupil's 'seeking an extraneous interest in a story as a story', as being more likely to hinder than help. An excellent summary of the contribution of such writers is given by Wardhaugh (1970). Wardhaugh elsewhere points out that the linguist, as a linguist, can only make his special contribution to the teaching of reading; there is no 'linguistic method of reading' as such – he can but add his insight to those of psychologists and educationalists: the total process must be interdisciplinary.

7. SUMMARY

The ability to read is largely dependent on the skill in the spoken language the learner already possesses; he has to recognize that visual signs represent the language he knows as sounds. The major reading skills are present in the oral language of young children: learning to read is a matter of drawing upon one's prior knowledge. The major reading skills we have been discussing are part of a general linguistic ability that we may characterize as an awareness of the possibilities of language.

SELECT READING LIST

The books and articles marked with an asterisk are suitable as an introduction to each topic.

LANGUAGE IN GENERAL (Chapters I and II)

*Quirk, R. (1962), *The Use of English* (Longmans, London). A clear, witty, authoritative book, which takes as its basis the practical everyday uses of English with which the general reader is familiar. There is a useful supplement on 'Notions of Correctness' by J. Warburg.

*Wilkinson, A. M. (1967), *In Your Own Words* (BBC Publications, 35 Marylebone High Street, London W.1). A short popular treatment, originally written for a TV series, on aspects of the spoken language, including accent, 'correct English', grammar, slang.

*Scargill, M. H., and Penner, P. G. (eds.), *Looking at Language.* Essays in Introductory Linguistics. Scott, Foresman & Co., Glenview, Illinois 60025. A simple accurate introduction to some basic topics in language.

Halliday, M. A. K., McIntosh, A., and Strevens, P. (1964), *The Linguistic Sciences and Language Teaching* (Longmans, London). An important and influential book in the tradition of British linguistics stemming from J. R. Firth. It considers the relationship of linguistics to language teaching, and gives a general exposition of scale-category grammar.

Robins, R. H. (1964), *General Linguistics: an Introductory Survey* (Longmans, London). A comprehensive work which will appeal mainly to the specialist student.

GRAMMAR (Chapter I)

*Mittins, W. H. (1962), *A Grammar of Modern English* (Methuen, London). A simple introduction to the subject, avoiding technicalities, and commitment to any particular school of thought, as far as possible; with useful illustrations and exercises.

*Roberts, P. (1962), *English Sentences* (Harcourt, Brace & World, New York). A simple exposition of the elements of transformational grammar.

Halliday, M. A. K., 'Categories of the Theory of Grammar', in *Word*, 17, 241–92. A difficult paper: a major statement of scale-category grammar.

Chomsky, N. (1957), *Synthetic Structures* (Mouton, The Hague). A very difficult book: a major statement of transformational grammar.

REGISTER (Chapter II)

*Strevens, P. (1965), *Papers in Language and Language Teaching*, Ch. 6, 'Varieties of English' (Oxford University Press). For articles on the *teaching* of register see papers by Brazil, Davies, Philp, in Wilkinson, A. M. (ed.), *The State of Language* (University of Birmingham School of Education, 1970).

SPOKEN ENGLISH (Chapter II)

*Wilkinson, A. M. (1965), *Spoken English*, with contributions by A. Davies and D. Atkinson (University of Birmingham School of Education. Obtainable from National Council of Teachers of English, Champaign, Ill.). A formulation of the concept of oracy, with papers on spoken English in schools and on listening.

THE ACQUISITION OF LANGUAGE (Chapter III)

*McNeill, D. (1966), 'The Creation of Language', in *Discovery*, 27, No. 7, 34–8; reprinted in Oldfield, R. C., and Marshall, J. C. (1968), *Language: Selected Readings* (Penguin, Harmondsworth, U.K.). McNeill explains LAD, the language acquisition device. A more elaborate presentation of the same title, with discussion by others, is given in Lyons, J., and Wales, R. J. (eds.) (1966), *Psycholinguistic Papers* (Edinburgh University Press).

Lewis, M. M. (1963), *Language, Thought and Personality in Infancy and Childhood* (Harrap, London). A standard work.

Bellugi, U., and Brown, R. W. (1964), *The Acquisition of Language* (Society for Research in Child Development, University of Chicago Press). The most important recent publication on the subject; papers, with discussion, on the development of grammar and the acquisition of syntax.

*Stones, E. (1966), Chapter on 'Language and Thought' in *An Introduction to Educational Psychology* (Methuen, London). Whorf, B. L. (1966), *Language, Thought, and Reality* (edited by J. B. Carroll (M.I.T. Press, Cambridge, Mass.). Whorf's collected papers form a classic statement of the way in which language may shape reality.

THE LANGUAGE ENVIRONMENT (Chapter V)

*May, F. B (1967), *Teaching Language as Communication to Children* (Chas. E. Merrill Books, Columbus, Ohio). Part I, 'Environmental Effects of Language Development', gives an excellent simple account of the effects of parents and siblings, cultural conditions and expectations, and school environment on children's linguistic development.

Lawton, D. (1968), *Social Class, Language, and Education* (Routledge & Kegan Paul, London). A survey of the research on the interrelationship of social factors and language, and a critique of the work of Bernstein; includes description of an experiment on restricted/elaborated codes.

CAPABILITY IN LANGUAGE (Chapter VI)

McCarthy, D. A. (1954), 'Language Development in Children', in Carmichael, L. (ed.), *A Manual of Child Psychology* (Wiley, New York), 492–630. This is an impressive survey of the research. A good deal of work has taken place since it was done, however, particularly under the influence of linguistics.

Carroll, J. B. (1968), 'Development of Native Language Skills Beyond the Early Years' (Educational Testing Service, Princeton, N.J.). To appear in a volume edited by C. Reed, *Language Learning* (National Council of Teachers of English, Champaign, Ill.). An excellent summary and evaluation of research; by far the best brief account available.

LINGUISTIC DISADVANTAGE (Chapter VII)

*Gulliford, R. (1969), *Backwardness and Educational Failure* National Foundation for Educational Research, Slough, U.K.). A short well-written introduction to the problem of disadvantage, with chapters on Language, Reading, Spelling, and Handwriting.

*Bernstein, Basil (1961), 'Social Structure, language and learning', *Educational Research, 3*. Bernstein's work on linguistic deprivation is fundamental. His ideas are evolving in a series of papers (see General Bibliography), but this one, written for teachers, seems to give the most representative single account.

CHILDREN'S USES OF LANGUAGE (Chapter VII)

Halliday, M. A. K. (1969), 'Relevant models of language', in Wilkinson, A. M. (ed.), *The State of Language* (University of Birmingham School of Education). An important paper which breaks new ground in its analysis of children's language in terms of functions rather than of its surface linguistic characteristics.

Dixon, J. (1967), 'Processes in Language Learning', Chapter 2 of *Growth Through English* (Oxford University Press).

Britton, James (1970), *Language and Learning* (Allen Lane).

READING (Chapter VIII, IX, X)

*Moyle, Donald (1968), *The Teaching of Reading* (Ward Lock Educational, London). There are many books on this topic. Moyle provides a clear comprehensive account of the theoretical and practical aspects.

*Southgate, V. and Roberts, G. R. (1970), *Reading – which Approach?* (University of London Press). A book of practical help for the teacher, who has to choose between a bewildering number of approaches; the main ones are surveyed with firm criteria in mind.

*Dakin, J. (1969), 'The Teaching of Reading', in Fraser H. and O'Donnell, W. R. (eds), *Applied Linguistics and the Teaching of English* (Longmans, London). A useful short account of the process from a linguistic viewpoint.

Fries, C. C. (1962), *Linguistics and Reading* (Holt, Rinehart & Winston, New York). Some of Fries's suggestions for practice are unattractive, but his theoretic statement (Ch. IV) of the transfer between oral language and reading is important.

Roberts, G. R. and Lunzer, E. A. (1968), 'Reading and Learning to Read', in the book edited by them, *Development in Human Learning* (Staples, London). An advanced account of current psycholinguistic thinking on the methods and learning processes involved.

GENERAL BIBLIOGRAPHY

Allen, R. V. and Allen C. (1967), *Language Experiences in Reading*, Teachers Resource Book, Level 3 (Encyclopaedia Britannica Press, Chicago).

Ames, L. B. and Walker, R. N. (1964), 'Prediction of later reading from Kindergarten Rorschach and I.Q. scores', *J.Ed.Psych.* 35, 309–15.

Anderson, I. H. and Dearborn, W. F. (1952), *The Psychology of Teaching Reading* (Ronald Press, New York).

Anon (18th cent.), *New England Primer* (Ginn & Co., Boston, Mass.). 20th cent. reprint.

Ashley, E. (n.d.), *The John and Mary Readers* (Schofield & Simms, Huddersfield).

Asker, W. (1923), 'Does knowledge of formal grammar function?', *School and Society* (27 Jan.), 109–11.

Austin, M. C. and Morrison, C. (1963), *The First R.: The Harvard Report on Reading in Elementary Schools* (MacMillan, New York).

Bagley, D. (1937), 'A critical study of objective estimates in the teaching of English', *Brit.J.Ed.Psych.* 7 (Feb.), 57–71; (June), 138–55.

Bailey, L. (1966). *Jamaican Creole Syntax* (Cambridge University Press).

Bellugi, U. and Brown, R. (1964), *The Acquisition of Language* (Monograph of the Society for Research in Child Development, University of Chicago Press).

Benfer, Mabel C. (1935). 'Sentence sense in relation to subject and predicate' (Master's thesis, University of Iowa).

Bereiter, C. and Engelmann, S. (1966), *Teaching Disadvantaged Children in the Preschool* (Prentice-Hall, New Jersey).

Bernstein, B. (1958), 'Some sociological determinants of perception', *Brit.J.Sociology*, 9, 159–74.

Bernstein, B. (1959), 'A public language: some sociological determinants of linguistic form', *Brit.J.Sociology*, 10, 311–26.

Bernstein, B. (1961), 'Social structure, language and learning', *Educational Research*, 3, 163–76.

Bernstein, B. (1962a), 'Linguistic codes, hesitation phenomena and intelligence', *Language and Speech*, 5, 31–45.

Bernstein, B. (1962b), 'Social class, linguistic codes and grammatical elements', *Language and Speech*, 5, 221–40.

Bernstein, B. (1964), 'Elaborated and Restricted codes: their origins and some consequences', in *Ethnography of Speech*, Monograph Issue of *American Anthropologist* (Mar. 1964).

Bernstein, B. (1969a), 'A socio-linguistic approach to socialisation, with some references to educability' (forthcoming).

Bernstein, B. (1969b), 'A critique of the concept of compensatory education', in Rubenstein, D. and Stoneman, C., *Education for Democracy* (Penguin, Harmondsworth, U.K.).

Bernstein, B. (1970), 'Education cannot compensate for society', New Society, 26 (Feb), 344–7.

Berry, M. (1971), *An Introduction to Systemic Linguistics* (Batsford).

Blank, M. and Solomon, F. (1968) 'A tutorial language programme to develop abstract thinking in socially disadvantaged pre-school children', *Child Development*, 39, 379–89.

Blatz, W. E., Fletcher, M. I., and Mason, M. (1937), 'Early development in spoken language of the Dionne quintuplets', in Blatz, W. E. *et al.*, *Collected Studies on the Dionne Quintuplets* (University of Toronto Studies in Child Development, No. 16).

Bloomfield, L. (1935), *Language* (George Allen & Unwin, London).

Bloomfield, L. and Barnhart, C. L. (1961), *Let's Read* (Wayne State University Press, Detroit).

Boraas, J. (1917), 'Formal grammar and the practical mastery of English' (Doctor's thesis, University of Minnesota).

Brook, G. L. (1963), *English Dialects* (André Deutsch, London).

Brown, R. and Bellugi, U. (1964), 'Three processes in the child's acquisition of syntax', in Lennenberg, E. H. (ed.), *New Directions in the Study of Language* (Massachusetts Institute of Technology, Cambridge, Mass.).

Brown, R. W. and Lennenberg, E. H. (1954), 'A study in language and cognition', *J. Abn. and Soc. Psych.* 49, 454–62.

Brown, R. W. and Ford, M. (1964), 'Address in American English', in Hymes, D. (ed.), *Language in Culture and Society* (Harper International, New York).

Burroughs, G. E. R. (1957), *A Study of the Vocabulary of Young Children* (University of Birmingham School of Education).

Burt, C. and Lewis, B. (1946), 'Teaching backward readers', *Brit.J.Ed.Psych.* 16, 116–32.

Carmichael, L. (ed.) (1954), *A Manual of Child Psychology* (John Wiley, New York).

Carroll, J. B. (1960), 'Language development', in Harris, C. W. (ed.), *Encyclopedia of Educational Research* (Macmillan, New York), 744–52.

Carroll, J. B. (1968), *Development of Native Language Skills beyond the Early Years* (Educational Testing Service, Princeton, N.J.).

Cartwright, D. and Jones, B. (1967), 'Further evidence relevant to the assessment of i.t.a.', *Educational Research*, 10, 65–71.

Carver, C. and Stowasser, C. H. (1964), *Oxford Colour Reading Books* (Oxford University Press, London).

Catherwood, C. (1932), 'A study of the relationship between a knowledge of rules and ability to correct grammatical errors and between identication of sentences and knowledge of subject and predicate' (Master's thesis, University of Minnesota).

Cherry, C. (1957), *On Human Communication* (M.I.T. Press, Cambridge, Mass.).

Chomsky, N. (1957), *Syntactic Structures* (Mouton, The Hague).

Chomsky, N. (1965), *Aspects of the Theory of Syntax* (M.I.T. Press, Cambridge, Mass.).

Chomsky, N. and Miller, G. A. (1963), 'Introduction to the formal analysis of natural languages', in Luce, R., Bush, R., and Galanter, E. (eds.), *Handbook of Mathematical Psychology* (Wiley, New York).

Coulthard, M. (1969), 'A discussion of restricted and elaborated codes', in Wilkinson, A. M. (ed.), *The State of Language* (University of Birmingham School of Education).

Dakin, J. (1969), 'The teaching of reading', in Fraser, H. and O'Donnell, W. R. (eds.), *Applied Linguistics and the Teaching of English* (Longmans, London).

Daniels, J. C. and Diack, H. (1954), *The Royal Road Readers* (Chatto & Windus, London).

Daniels, J. C. and Diack, H. (1956), *Progress in Reading* (Nottingham University Institute of Education).

Daniels, J. C. and Diack, H. (1958), *Progress in Reading in the Infant School* (Nottingham University Institute of Education).

Davis, E. A. (1937), 'The development of linguistic skill in twins, singletons with siblings, and only children from age five to ten years' (Institute of Child Welfare, Monograph Series No. 14, University of Minnesota Press, Minneapolis).

Day, E. J. (1932), 'The development of language in twins; 1: A comparison of twins and single children', *Child Development*, 3, 179–99.

Diack, H. (1960), *Reading and the Psychology of Perception* (Skinner, London).

Dixon, R. M. W. (1965), *What is Language? A New Approach to Linguistic Description* (Longmans, London).

Dolch, E. W. (1951), *Psychology and the Teaching of Reading* (The Garrard Press, Champaign, Ill.).

Dolch, E. W. (n.d.), *Teaching Primary Reading*, 2nd edn. (The Garrard Press, Champaign, Ill.).

Downing, J. A. (1964), *The i.t.a Reading Experiment* (Evans Bros., London; Scott, Foresman, Chicago).

Downing, J. and Jones, B. (1966), 'Some problems of evaluating i.t.a.: A second experiment, *Educational Research*, 8, 100–14.

Ervin, S. M. and Miller, W. R. (1963), 'Language development', in Stevenson, H. W. *et al.* (eds.), *Child Psychology* 62nd *Yearbook*, Part 1 (National Society for the Study of Education).

Firth, J. R. (1959), 'The Treatment of Language in General Linguistics' *The Medical Press*, 19th August.

Fraser, C., Bellugi, U., and Brown, R. (1963), 'Control of grammar in imitation, comprehension, and production', *J.Verb.Learn. Verb.Behav.* 2, 121–35. This essay is reprinted in Oldfield and Marshall (1968).

Fraser, H. and O'Donnell, W. R. (eds.) (1969), *Applied Linguistics and the Teaching of English* (Longmans, London).

Freeberg, N. E. and Payne, D. T. (1967), 'Parental influence on cognitive development in early childhood,' a review in *Child Development*, 38, 65–87.

Fries, C. C. (1962), *Linguistics & Reading* (Holt, Rinehart & Winston, New York).

Fries, C. C. (1963), *The Structure of English* (Longmans, London).

Fry, E. (1964), 'A diacritical marking system to aid beginning reading instruction', *Elementary English* (May).

Gates, A. I. (1935), *A Reading Vocabulary for Primary Grades* (Bureau of Publications, Teachers' College, Columbia University, New York).

Gattegno, C. (1962), *Words in Colour* (Educational Explorers Ltd., Reading, U.K.).

Giles, H. (1970), 'Evaluative reactions to accents', *Educational Review*, 22, 2.

Goldfarb, W. (1945), 'Effects of psychological deprivation in infancy and subsequent stimulation', *Amer.J.Psychiat.* 102, 18–33.

Goldfarb, W. (1943), 'The effects of early institutional care on adolescent personality', *J.Exp.Educ.* 12, 106–29.

Goodacre, E. J. (1966), *Reading in Infant Classes* (National Foundation for Educational Research, Slough, U.K.).

Graham, N. C. and Gulliford, R. (1968), 'A psycholinguistic approach to the language deficiencies of educationally subnormal children', in Wilkinson, A. M. (ed.), *The Place of Language*, special issue of *Educational Review*, 20, No. 2. 136–45.

Gray, L. S. (1956), *The Teaching of Reading and Writing* (UNESCO Monograph on Fundamental Education, X, 1956).

Gregory, M. (1967), 'Aspects of variety differentiation', *Journal of Linguistics*, 3, No. 2, 177–98.

Gregory, R. E. (1965), 'Unsettledness, maladjustment, and reading failure: a village study', *Brit.J.Ed.Psych.* 35, 63–8.

Gurney, P. (1965), *The Foundling* (Premio Italia per un'opera radio stereofonica, Firenze, 27 Septembre). BBC Italia Prize-winning play.

Hall, A., Jr. (1964), *Introductory Linguistics* (Chilton Co., Philadelphia).

Halliday, M. A. K., McIntosh, A., and Strevens, P. (1964), *The Linguistic Sciences and Language Teaching* (Longmans, London).

Halliday, M. A. K. (1969), 'Relevant models of language', in Wilkinson, A. M. (ed.), *The State of Language* (University of Birmingham School of Education).

Harley, R. K. (1963), *Verbalism Among Blind Children: an Investigation and Analysis* (American Association for the Blind, New York).

Hattwick, B. W. and Stowell, M. (1936), 'The relation of parental over-attentiveness to children's work habits and social adjustments in kindergarten and the first six grades of school', *Journal of Educational Research*, 30, 169.

Hawkins, P. R. (1969), 'Social class, the nominal group and reference', *Language and Speech*, 12, 125–35.

Heath, W. G. (1962), 'Library-centred English', *Educational Review*, 14, 2.

Herbert, A. J. (1965), *The Structure of Technical English* (Longmans, London).

Hess, R. D. and Shipman, V. C. (1965), 'Early experience and the socialisation of cognitive modes in children', *Child Development*, 36 (4), 869–86.

Higgenbotham, D. C. (1961), 'A study of the speech of kindergarten, first and second grade children in audience situations, with particular attention to maturation and learning, as evidenced in content, forms, and delivery' (Doctoral dissertation, Northwestern University, Evanston, Ill.).

Hildreth, G. (1958), *Teaching Reading* (Holt, Rinehart & Winston, New York).

Houghton, V. P. (1967), '"Why Dyslexia?", in Downing, J. and Brown, A. L., *The Second International Reading Symposium* (Cassell, London).

Howard, R. W. (1946), 'The language development of a group of triplets', *J. Genet. Psych*. 69, 181–8.

Huey, E. B. (1912), *The Psychology and Pedagogy of Reading* (Macmillan, New York).

Ingram, E. (1969), 'Language development in children', in Fraser, H. and O'Donnell, W. R. (eds.), *Applied Linguistics and the Teaching of English* (Longmans, London).

Jackson, H. L. (1969), *Sex Differences in English Performance* (Moray House, Edinburgh).

Jones, K. J. (1967), 'Comparing i.t.a with *Colour Story Reading*', *Educational Research*, 10, 226–34.

Jones, K. J. (1967), *Colour Story Reading* (Nelson, London).

Joos, M. (1962), *The Five Clocks* (Mouton, The Hague).

Keir, G. (1951), *Adventures in Reading* (Oxford University Press, London).

Kirk, S. A. (1966), *The Diagnosis and Remediation of Psycholinguistic Abilities* (University of Illinois Press, Urbana, Ill.).

Kirk and McCarthy, J. J. have developed from this the *Illinois Test of Psycho-linguistic Abilities.*

Labov, W. (1964). 'Stages in the acquisition of standard English', in Shuy, R. W. (ed.), *Social Dialects and Language Learning* (National Council of Teachers of English (USA), Champaign, Ill.).

Lawton, D. (1968), Social Class, Language and Education (Routledge & Kegan Paul, London).

Lee, T. (1967), 'Writing and talking: an appraisal of *Words in Colour, Current Research and Practice: Proceedings of the United Kingdom Reading Association,* 1 (1966–7).

Lefevre, C. A. (1964), *Linguistics and the Teaching of Reading* (McGraw-Hill, New York).

Lewis, M. M. (1963), *Language, Thought and Personality in Infancy and Childhood* (Harrap, London).

Lewis, M. M. (1968), *Language and Personality in Deaf Children* (National Foundation for Educational Research, Slough, U.K.).

Lippitt, R. and White, R. K. (1958), 'An experimental study of leadership and group life', in Maccoby, E. E. et al. (eds.), *Readings in Social Psychology* (Holt, Rinehart & Winston, New York).

Loban, W. D. (1963), *The Language of Elementary School Children* (Research Report No. 1, National Council of Teachers of English, 508 South Sixth Street, Champaign, Ill.).

Loban, W. D. (1966), *Problems in Oral English, Kindergarten Through Grade Nine* (National Council of Teachers of English, Champaign, Ill.).

Lunzer, E. A. and Roberts, G. R. (1968), 'Reading and learning to read', in Lunzer, E. A. and Morris, J. F. (eds.), *Development in Human Learning,* Vol. 2 (Staples Press, London).

Lyman, R. L. (1929), *Summary of Investigations Relating to Grammar, Language and Composition* (University of Chicago Press).

Maccauley, W. J. (1947), 'The difficulty of grammar', *Brit.J.Ed. Psych.* 17 (Nov.), 153–62.

MacKay, D., Thompson, B., and Schaub, P. (1970), *Breakthrough to Literacy,* Teacher's Manual (Longmans, London).

Malmstrom, J. and Ashley, A. (1963), *Dialects U.S.A.* (National Council of Teachers of English, Champaign, Ill.).

Malmquist, E. (1958), *Reading Disabilities in the First Grade of the Elementary School* (Almquist & Wilksell, Stockholm).

Martin, C. (1955), 'Developmental inter-relationships among language variables in children of first grade', *Elementary English*, 3, No. 2 (Mar.), 167–71.

Maxfield, K. E. (1936), 'The spoken language of the blind pre-school child: a study of methods', *Archives of Psychology*, No. 201 (May).

McCarthy, D. (1930), *The Language Development of the Pre-school Child* (Institute of Child Welfare Monograph, Set. No. 4, University of Minnesota Press, Minneapolis).

McCarthy, D. A. (1954), 'Language development in children', in Carmichael, L. (ed.), *A Manual of Child Psychology* (John Wiley, New York), 492–630.

McDavid, R. I., Jr. (1967), 'A checklist of significant features for discriminating social dialects', in Everetts, E. L. (ed.), *Dimensions of Dialect* (National Council of Teachers of English, Champaign, Ill.).

McNally, J. and Murray, W. (1962), *Key Words to Literacy* (Schoolmaster Publishing Co., London).

McNamara, J. (1966), *Bilingualism and Primary Education: a Study of Irish Experience* (Edinburgh University Press).

McNeill, D. (1966), 'The creation of language', *Discovery*, 27, No. 7, 34–8. Reprinted in Oldfield and Marshall (1968).

Menyuk, P. (1963), 'A preliminary evaluation of grammatical capacity in children', *J.Verb.Learn.Verb.Behav.* 2, 429–39.

Menyuk, P. (1964), 'Alteration of rules in children's grammar', *J.Verb.Learn.Verb.Behav.* 3, 480–8.

Merritt, J (1969), 'Reading skills re-examined', *Special Education* (U.K.), 58, No. 1 (Mar.).

Miles, T. R. (1967), 'In defence of the concept of dyslexia', in Downing, J. and Brown, A. L., *The Second International Reading Symposium* (Cassell, London).

Miller, G. A. (1963), *Language and Communication* (McGraw-Hill, New York).

Mittins, W. H. (1969), 'What is correctness?' in Wilkinson, A. M. (ed.), *The State of Language* (University of Birmingham School of Education).

Moore, J. K. (1947), 'Speech content of selected groups of orphan-age and non-orphanage pre-school children,' *J.Exp.Educ.* 16, 122–33.

Morris, J. M. (1966), *Standards and Progress in Reading* (National Foundation for Educational Research, Slough, U.K.).

Murray, W. (1964), *The Key Words Reading Scheme* (Wills & Hepworth, Loughborough, U.K.).

Noel, D. L. (1953), 'A comparative study of the relationship between the quality of the child's language usage and the quality and types of language used in the home', *Educational Research*, 47 (Nov.), 161–7.

O'Donnell, R., Griffin, W. J., and Norris, R. C. (1967), *Syntax of Kindergarten and Elementary School Children: a Transformational Analysis* (National Council of Teachers of English, Champaign, Ill.).

Oldfield, R. C. and Marshall. J. C. (1968), *Language: Selected Readings* (Penguin, Harmondsworth, U.K.).

Opie, I. and Opie, P. (1951), *The Oxford Dictionary of Nursery Rhymes* (Oxford University Press, London).

Piaget, J. (1968), *Six Psychological Studies*, with an Introduction, Notes, and Glossary by D. Elkind; translated by A. Tenzer (University of London Press).

Piaget, J. and Inhelder, B. (1969), *The Psychology of the Child*; translated by H. Weaver (Routledge, London).

Potter, S. (1968), revision of Bradley, H., *The Making of English* (Macmillan, London).

Pressey, S. L. and Robinson, F. P. (1944), *Psychology and the New Education*, 2nd edn. (Harper, New York).

Ramsey, W. (1962), 'An evaluation of three methods of teaching sixth grade reading', *Challenge and Experiment in Reading: International Reading Association Conference Proceedings*, 7.

Rankin, E. (1969), 'Report of problems relating to the teaching of the mother tongue: Scotland' (UNESCO First Language Learning Seminar, Hamburg, Dec. 1969). The Seminar Report is to be published.

Reynell, J. K. (1969), *Reynell Developmental Language Scales* (National Foundation for Educational Research, Slough, U.K.).

Rice, J. M. (1903–4), 'Educational research: the results of a test in language & English', *Forum*, XXXV, 209–93, 440–57.

Rickard, G. E. (1935), 'The recognition vocabulary of primary pupils', *Journal of Educational Research*, 29, 281–91.

Roberts, P. (1962), *English Sentences* (Harcourt, Brace & World, New York).

Robins, R. H. (1964), *General Linguistics: an Introductory Survey* (Longmans, London).

Robinson, H. M. (1949), *Manifestations of Emotional Maladjustment in Reading* (Supplementary Educational Monographs, No. 68, University of Chicago Press), 114–22.

Robinson, N. (1960), 'The relationship between knowledge of English grammar and ability in English composition', *Brit.J.Ed. Psych.* 30, 184–6.

Ruddell, R. B. (1965), 'The effects of oral and written patterns of language structure on reading comprehension', International Reading Association, *The Reading Teacher* (Jan.).

Russell, D. M. (1961), *Children Learning to Read* (Ginn & Co., Boston, Mass.).

Russell, D. M. and Fea, H. F. (1963), papers in Gage, N. L. (ed.), *Handbook of Research on Teaching* (Rand, McNally & Co., New York).

Ryans, D. G. (1961), 'Some relationships between pupil behaviour and certain teacher characteristics' *Brit.J.Ed.Psych.* 52. 82–90.

Sapir, Edward (1921), *Language: An Introduction to the Study of Speech* (Harcourt, Brace & World, New York).

Saussure, F. de (1961), *Course in General Linguistics*, edited by C. Bally, and A. Sechehaye, in collaboration with A. Reidlinger; translated by W. Baskin (Owen, London).

Scarborough, O. R. *et al.* (1961), 'Anxiety level and performance in school subjects', *Psychological Reports*, 9, 425.

Schonell, F. J. (1945), *The Psychology and Teaching of Reading* (Oliver and Boyd, Edinburgh).

Sears, I. and Diebel, A. (1916), 'A study of common mistakes in pupils' oral English', *Elementary School Journal* (USA) (Sept.), 44–54.

Segal, D. and Barr, N. R. (1926), 'Relation and achievement in formal grammar to achievement in applied grammar', *Educational Research*, 14, 401–2.

Shannon, C. E. (1949), *The Mathematical Theory of Communication* (University of Illinois Press, Urbana, Ill).

Sinclair, J. McH. (1971), *A Course in Spoken English: Part Three, Grammar* (Oxford University Press, London).

Skull, J. (1968), 'The Construction of an Oral Composition Scale at the C.S.E. level, and an analysis of some of the linguistic features in the Compositions' (unpublished M.Ed. thesis, University of Birmingham).

Southgate, V. (1965), 'Approaching i.t.a. results with caution', *Educational Research*, 7, No. 2, 83–96.

Southgate, V. (1966), 'A few comments on "Reading Drive"', *Educational Research*, 9, 145–6.

Slobin, D. J. (1966), 'Grammatical transformations and sentence comprehension in childhood and adulthood', *J.Verb.Learn. Verb.Behav.* 5, 219–27.

Smith, M. E. (1935), 'A study of some of the factors influencing the development of the sentence in pre-school children', *J.Genet. Psych.* 46, 182–212.

Smith, K. (1941), 'Measurement of the size of general English vocabulary through the elementary grades and high school' *Genetic Psychology Monographs*, 24, 311–45.

Spearritt, D. (1962), *Listening Comprehension: a Factorial Analysis* (Australian Council for Education Research).

Spencer, J. W. and Gregory, M. J. (1964), 'An approach to the study of style', in Enkvist, N. E., Spencer, J. W., and Gregory, M. J. (1964), *Linguistics and Style* (Oxford University Press, London).

Squire, J. C. and Applebee, R. K. (1969), *Teaching English in the United Kingdom* (National Council of Teachers of English (USA), Champaign, Ill.).

Stewart, W. A. (1964), 'Negro speech: socio-linguistic factors affecting English teaching', in Shuy, R. W. (ed.), *Social Dialects and Language Learning* (National Council of Teachers of English, Champaign, Ill.).

Stones, E. (1966), *An Introduction to Educational Psychology* (Methuen, London).

Stott, D. H. (1962), *The Programmed Reading Kit* (W. & R. Holmes, London).

Stott, D. H. (1964), *Roads to Literacy* (W. & R. Holmes, London).

Strang, B. (1962), *Modern English Structure* (Edward Arnold, London).

Strevens, P. D. (1965), 'Varieties of English, Chapter 6, in *Papers in Language and Language Teaching* (Oxford University Press, London).

Strickland, R. G. (1962), 'The language of elementary school children; its relationship to the language of reading text books and the quality of reading of selected children', *Bulletin of the School of Education, Indiana University*, 38, No. 4 (July 1962).

Stutsman, R. (1931), *Mental Measurement of Pre-school Children* (World Books, Tarry Town-on Hudson, USA), Merrill-Palmer Scale: 18 months – 6 years. Both verbal and non-verbal.

Symonds, P. M. (1931), 'Practice vs. grammar in the learning of correct usage', *J.Ed.Psych.* 22, 81–96.

Templin, M. C. (1957), *Certain Language Skills in Children: their Development and Inter-relationships* (University of Minnesota Press, Minneapolis).

Terman, L. M. and Merrill, M. A. (1960), *The Stamford-Binet Test, Form LM* (Harrap, London: Houghton Mifflin, New York).

Thomas, O. (1965), *Transformational Grammar and the Teaching of English* (Holt, Rinehart & Winston, New York).

Thorndike, E. L. (1944), *Teacher's Word Book of 30,000 Words* (Bureau of Publications, Teachers' College, Columbia University, New York).

Tillman, M. H. (1967), 'The factor structure of verbal abilities of blind and sighted children' (paper at American Educational Research Association Annual Meeting).

Tillman, M. H. and Williams, C. (1968), 'Word associations of blind and sighted children to selected form classes' (paper at American Educational Research Association Annual Meeting, University of Georgia).

Vernon, M. D. (1967), 'Review of recent research on backwardness in reading', in Downing, J. and Brown, A. L. (eds.), *The Second International Reading Symposium* (Cassell, London).

Vygotsky, L. S. (1965), *Thought and Language*; translated by Hanfman and Vakar (Massachusetts Institute of Technology, Cambridge, Mass.).

Warburg, J. (1962), 'Notions of correctness', in Quirk, R., *The Use of English* (Longmans, London).

Warburton, F. W. and Southgate, V (1969), *i.t.a.: an Independent Evaluation* (John Murray/W. & R. Chambers, Edinburgh).

Wardhaugh, R. (1969), *Reading: a Linguistic Perspective* (Harcourt, Brace & World, New York).

Weir, R. H. (1962), *Language in the Crib* (Mouton, The Hague).

Weschler, D. (1967), *The Weschler Pre-School and Primary Scale of Intelligence* (WISC – Weschler Intelligence Scale for Children (Psychological Corporation, New York).

Whorf, B. L. (1966), *Language, Thought and Reality*, edited by

J. B. Carroll (Massachusetts Institute of Technology, Cambridge, Mass.).

Wijk, A. (1959), *Regularized Inglish* (Almqvist & Wiksell, Stockholm).

Wilkinson, A. M. (ed.) (1958), *Songs of Innocence and of Experience by William Blake* (University Tutorial Press, London).

Wilkinson, A. M. (1965), *Spoken English*, with contributions by A. Davies and D. Atkinson (University of Birmingham School of Education. Obtainable from National Council of Teachers of English, Champaign, Ill.).

Wilkinson, A. M. (ed.) (1966), *Some Aspects of Oracy* (National Association for the Teaching of English (U.K.). Obtainable from N.C.T.E., Champaign, Ill.).

Wilkinson, A. M. (1968), 'The Implications of Oracy', in Wilkinson, A. M. (ed.), *The Place of Language* (University of Birmingham School of Education).

Wilkinson, A. M. (1969), 'The quality of language experience in younger children', *J. of Curric. Studies*, 1, No. 3 (Nov.)

Wilkinson, A. M. (1969), 'Oral Constraints and Reading Acquisition' in Wilkinson, A. M. (ed.), *The State of Language*, University of Birmingham School of Education.

Wilkinson, A. M. and Stratta, L. (1970), 'Listening comprehension at thirteen plus', *Educational Review*, 22, 228–42.

Wilkinson, A. M. (1970), 'Research in listening comprehension', *Educational Research*, 12, No. 2.

GLOSSARY AND INDEX

My comments on _____ Author or Editor _____ Title

Date _____ Name of course _____

You may quote me _____ Possible Adoption? Yes ___ No ___

Please do not quote me _____ Approx. course enrollment? _____

Name (please print) _____

Dept. _____ Position _____

Institution _____

City _____ State _____ Zip code _____

pics ✓

"A vivid evocation of the blood and guts, not to mention sheer guts, that marked the original Olympic Games more than two thousand years ___ T___ P_____ tells the gripping story of a festival of physi_____ _____ _____ _____ ometimes lost, ____ _____ _____ _____

and Times
of Rome's Greatest Politician

"Fans of Tony Perrottet's *Pagan Holiday* (aka *Route 66 A.D.*) will kill to read his follow-up, *The Naked Olympics*. A seasoned traveller, Perrottet follows all the highways and byways of ancient Olympic lore. He really makes you feel what it was like to be at the ancient Olympics, conjuring up the sights, sounds, smells (especially the smells) of the Games with a sure and vivid touch. *The Naked Olympics* would be just the thing to cover your nakedness as you watch the 2004 Athens Olympics or go to visit the ancient site of Olympia—fig leaves need not apply."

—PAUL CARTLEDGE, Professor of Classics,
Cambridge University, and author of *The Spartans*

"*The Naked Olympics* presents the Greeks in all their glory, brutality, and vulgarity. It is a fascinating picture and popular history at its best." —NORMAN F. CANTOR, Professor Emeritus,
New York University, and author of *Antiquity:*
The Civilization of the Ancient World

"I considered myself a pretty solid researcher on ancient Greece, till Tony Perrottet's *The Naked Olympics* blew me out of the water. I never knew (just two among hundreds of delicious factoids) that there was no separate event for discus and javelin—they were part of the pentathlon—or that the chariot race ran twenty-four laps and took fifteen hair-raising minutes. (Not to mention the distinction between various attendant types of groupies, courtesans, and *pornai*.) Mr. Perrottet's vivid cinematic prose not only delivers encyclopedic intelligence of the ancient games but spirits you back in time with such immediacy that you can smell the sweat and feel the hot Greek sun. If you're going to be glued to the modern Athens Games like I will, you must read *The Naked Olympics*. No other book communicates 'where it all came from' with such authenticity."

—STEVEN PRESSFIELD, author of *Gates of Fire*,
Tides of War, and *Last of the Amazons*

"This is the book to read if you want to know what it felt like to be a spectator or a contestant at the ancient Olympic Games. Perrottet brings the scene to life in all its pageantry and squalor, with its beautiful bodies, rotting meat, flies, and broiling heat. Then, as now, the games brought out the best and the worst of human potential, and blood, sweat, tears, sex, and money were all part of the Olympic experience, along with religion, bribery, and politics."

—MARY LEFKOWITZ, the Andrew W. Mellon Professor
in the Humanities at Wellesley College and author of
Greek Gods, Human Lives: What We Can Learn from Myths

"Short of building your own time machine, reading Tony Perrottet's *The Naked Olympics* will be the closest you'll come to experiencing the blood, sweat, glory, and greed that were the ancient Olympic Games. And if you do somehow happen upon a time machine, you'd still be wise to trust Tony Perrottet as your guide. Steeped in scholarship, leavened by humor, and lighted by the same flames of history and love of sport that illuminated the works of Homer, Lucian, Herodotus, Thucydides, Pausanias, and Dio the Golden-Tongued, Perrottet's *The Naked Olympics: The True Story of the Ancient Games* is one of those rare books that you'll be citing for years to come."   —DAN SIMMONS, author of *Ilium*

"Erudite, colorful, and frequently hilarious, Perrottet's *The Naked Olympics* is a marvelous resource for athletes, spectators, and scholars alike. I will never watch the Olympic games in quite the same way again."   —MICHAEL CURTIS FORD, author of
The Ten Thousand and *The Last King*